PROGRES
SCHOO
EXERCISES

for

DRESSAGE & JUMPING

PROGRESSIVE SCHOOL EXERCISES

for

DRESSAGE & JUMPING

A Handbook for Instructors and Riders

ISLAY AUTY BA, FBHS

KENILWORTH PRESS

I dedicate this book to the following people:

my late parents, Euan and Bunny Dawson, without whose unfailing support I would never have entered an equine career;

Janet Sturrock FHBS, under whose training and then lifelong friendship I developed much of the coaching philosophy that I value today;

lastly, but most importantly, my wonderful husband David and son Robert, who have constantly supported me throughout the days and years, when I have often given more time to the horses than was justified.

Published in Great Britain by
Kenilworth Press Ltd
Addington, Buckingham, MK18 2JR

First published 2001
Reprinted 2002

British Library Cataloguing in Publication Data
A catalogue record for this book is available from the British Library.

ISBN 1-872119-38-7

Layout and typesetting by Kenilworth Press
Diagrams by Michael J. Stevens
Main cover illustration by Dianne Breeze
Cover design by Alyson Kyles

Printed and bound in Great Britain by Bell & Bain

CONTENTS

About this book 7
Teaching notes 8

PART ONE – WORK ON THE FLAT

LOOPS AND CIRCLES

Simple loops 10
Small serpentine loops 12
More demanding loops 14
Developing loops and circles 16
More small circles 18

CIRCLES WITH TRANSITIONS

20m circle and transitions 20
Circles large and small 22
Satellite circles 24
Concentric circles 26
Shortening and lengthening on circles 28

DIAGONAL LINES

Using short diagonal lines 30
Developing the short diagonal exercise 32

MOVING AWAY FROM THE LEG

Improving corners with halt transitions 34
Halts with turn on the forehand 36
More turns on the forehand 38
Work towards walk pirouettes 40

INTRODUCING LEG YIELD

Simple leg yielding 42
Centre line leg yielding 44
More centre line leg yielding 46
Leg yield on the diagonal line 48

MORE DEMANDING LEG YIELD EXERCISES

Diagonal leg yield with a transition 50
Leg yield with half circles 52
Leg yield and turn on the forehand 54
Leg yield with canter 56

DEVELOPING CANTER

Transitions using canter 58
Introducing counter canter 60
More counter canter 62

SHOULDER-IN

Introducing shoulder-in 64
Shoulder-in and lengthen 66
Shoulder-in with transition 68
Shoulder-in away from the wall 70

PART TWO – JUMPING EXERCISES

Introduction 74
Basic grid 76
Grid with a bounce 78
Developing the bounce grid 80
Centre line zigzag 82
Grid progressions 84
Doubles in trot and canter 86
The 'cover-all' exercise 88
Two-jump circle 90
Simple related distances and 'dogleg' 92

ABOUT THIS BOOK

This book has been compiled to offer more advanced school exercises and movements for:

- all levels of teacher, whether involved in training groups or individuals;
- riders schooling their own horses or ponies;
- anyone interested, for whatever reason, in furthering his repertoire of work for riders and horses.

The book is divided into:

(a) exercises on the flat;

(b) exercises over fences.

These two sections are subdivided into groups of exercises which are similar, or have progressive components (i.e. a simple exercise building into a more complex format). Cross-references are given where an exercise could usefully fall into more than one group.

Each exercise featured contains the following:

- general notes about the exercise with a description of its 'floor plan';
- an explanation of the aims and benefits of the exercise;
- preparation;
- aids and execution;
- relevant points on teaching the exercise;
- possible faults or problems.

Most of the exercises can be ridden in a 20m x 40m school, though some are more suitable for a 20m x 60m school.

The **flatwork exercises** in this book are directed at the horse (or pony) who is already secure in his basic training. He should be able to:

- move genuinely forward when asked, in the three basic gaits – walk, trot and canter;
- accept the basic aids of seat, legs and hands, supported by relevant use of the voice, usually as a reward; a schooling whip and/or spurs are further aids which the trained or half-trained horse may have encountered;
- maintain rhythm (regularity) in all three gaits;
- accept the bit quietly and confidently as a result of activity of the hind legs, through a supple back to an elastic connection in the mouth;
- move 'straight' on straight lines, and on curves and circles: i.e. the hind legs following the track of the forelegs, with suppleness through the horse's frame;
- work enthusiastically in an unconstrained way, the paces showing a lively freedom and elasticity unhindered by stiffness or tension.

The same basic training requirements set out above apply to the horse attempting the **jumping exercises** in the second section of the book. The better the horse's balance and coordination in his work on the flat, the more able he will be to use his athleticism for jumping. Ultimately a horse's jumping ability is dictated or limited by his scope and desire to jump fences. The horse who is well schooled on the flat, obedient and supple, will be far more equipped to develop his jumping skills and therefore his confidence, than the horse whose basic training is lacking. The latter type of horse will often jump bravely until his lack of training causes a problem (e.g. lack of balance or rhythm in the paces), which may lead to the horse hitting his fences and subsequently losing his confidence.

TEACHING NOTES

The role of the teacher, instructor or coach is:

- to impart knowledge;
- to convey clear and orthodox (acceptable) doctrine (policy);
- to develop skill and build confidence;
- as a result of assessment, to be able to choose appropriate work for the pupil(s);
- to develop work progressively, maintaining the confidence of the pupil(s);
- to present information in an interesting way to stimulate and motivate learning;
- to recognise weaknesses and in so doing, accentuate the positive, working to eliminate the negative;
- to plan progressively, allowing the pupil to recognise achievable goals;
- to discuss and set goals for short-, medium- and long-term aims – those goals to be realistic and measurable;
- to offer relevant encouragement, support and praise as appropriate to the pupil(s) and close associates (e.g. parents) from which future work can be planned;
- to be aware of the factors which may affect learning (e.g. rider fitness, mental state, environment, weather, outside influences).

The teacher must have:

- knowledge of the subject;
- interest in imparting the knowledge;
- loyalty and integrity;
- enthusiasm;
- good communication skills;
- stamina;
- reliability;
- authority.

PART ONE

WORK ON THE FLAT

SIMPLE LOOPS

Arena
20 x 40m or
20 x 60m

Gaits
walk, trot and canter

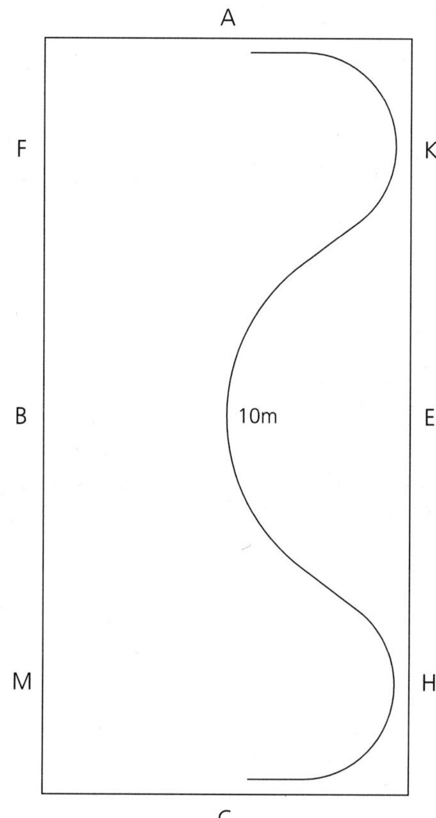

ABOUT THIS EXERCISE

- The loop leaves the track at the first quarter marker after the corner leaving the short side of the arena.
- The horse's bend is changed over the deepest part of the loop opposite E or B.
- The bend is then changed again on returning to the quarter marker before the next short side.
- These loops can and should be ridden on both reins.
- The bend should be even throughout the horse's body.
- The hind legs should follow the same line (track) as the front legs.
- The exercise may be ridden in **walk**, **trot** or **canter**. However, if ridden in **canter** the exercise is **more demanding** because it involves some counter canter.
- **If ridden in canter**: the centre of the loop is in counter canter, i.e. the horse maintains the bend over the leading leg and the bend is not changed. This requires greater balance and engagement from the horse and therefore is a more advanced suppling and straightening exercise. Start with shallow loops (2–3m) and build up to deeper loops as the horse's balance and ability develop.
- Throughout the loop, rhythm, balance, smoothness and harmony are the priorities.

AIMS AND BENEFITS

- To improve the lateral suppleness of the horse.

- To encourage the horse to accept the aids evenly on both sides, through the changes of direction.
- To develop equal elasticity of both sides of the horse's body.
- To ensure maintenance of rhythm, balance and suppleness through frequent changes of direction.

PREPARATION

- Establish rhythm and forwardness in the gait.
- Think ahead, look ahead and ride as deeply into the corners as the horse's balance and coordination will allow.
- Make sure that the horse is listening and 'in front of the leg', i.e. instantly ready and willing to obey the aids to go forward.
- Maintain a good, balanced position so that aid application is clear.

AIDS AND EXECUTION

- Ridden in walk, rising or sitting trot: the inside leg on the girth maintains impulsion; the outside leg a little behind the girth controls the hindquarters. The inside rein gives slight direction to the horse by creating a little flexion into the first part of the loop. The outside rein regulates that degree of flexion and controls the pace.
- In canter care must be taken to sustain these aids consistently in balance, with the bend of the leading leg, irrespective of the direction.
- The aids guide the horse off the track and as he reaches the deepest part of the loop, a smooth change of the aids directs the horse into the new bend, e.g. if the loop is ridden on the right rein, in the first part of the loop, the inside hand and leg are the **right** hand and leg, the outside hand and leg are the **left** hand and leg.
- Over the deepest part of the loop the aids are reversed, and then as the final part of the loop returns to the track, the aids revert to the original ones again.

RELEVANT TEACHING POINTS

- The exercise should be ridden smoothly.
- Sufficient energy – forward movement – will facilitate a more fluent result.
- The rider may need help to gauge the depth of the loop: 5m is half way to the centre line; 10m is to the centre line, which would be to X at the deepest point.
- Riding a good corner before and after the loop helps develop and maintain accuracy and engagement.
- The aids must be changed smoothly but clearly so that the resulting change of bend is fluent.
- 'Inside' and 'outside' when referring to the rider's aids always relate to the direction in which the horse is bent, **never** to the inside or outside of the arena.
- An excellent initial warming-up and suppling exercise.
- Practice of the figure will gradually instil competence.

FAULTS

- The horse may bend easily one way but bend reluctantly or not at all the other way. This indicates the horse's 'hollow' or easy side and his stiff side.
- On the stiff side, there may be little or no lateral bend or suppleness. The rider must persevere and use his inside leg more energetically to activate the horse's lazy inside hind leg.
- The horse may stiffen and lose rhythm and/or impulsion on the stiff side.
- The rider may allow the horse to have too much bend in the neck on the 'hollow' side. If so, the horse's weight will then travel through the outside shoulder and the 'straightness' will be lost.
- The rider may misjudge the shape or size of the loop.

SMALL SERPENTINE LOOPS

Arena
20 x 40m or
20 x 60m

Gait
walk

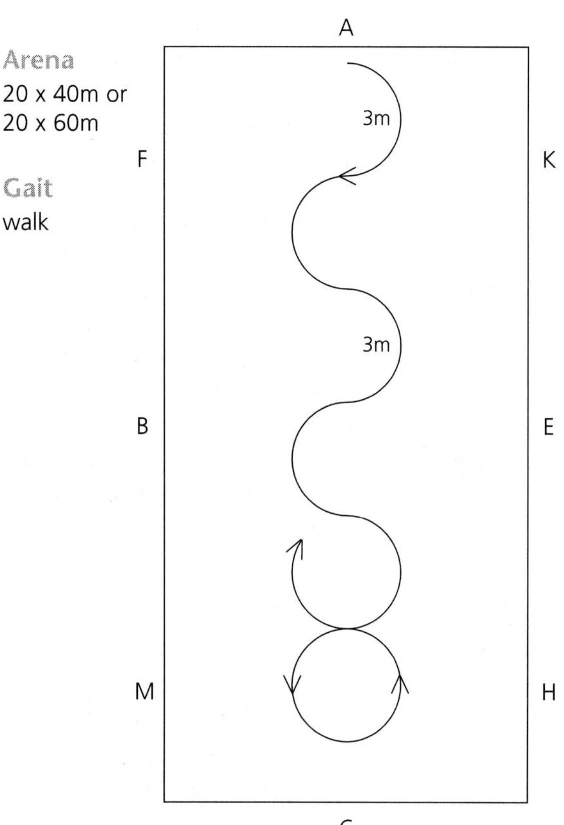

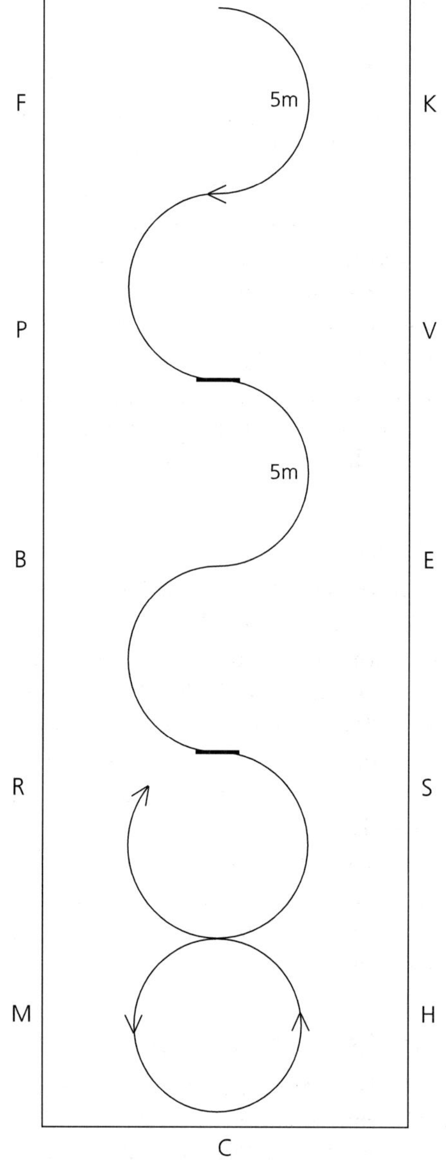

ABOUT THIS EXERCISE

- This exercise is very helpful at the beginning of a horse's work to aid suppleness and prepare him for work.
- For this purpose it is most usefully carried out in **walk**.
- Similarly it can be used to loosen the rider and begin to allow him to think about effective aid application.
- It can be performed by a group of riders working in open order provided that the centre line is ridden in one direction only.
- If used as an exercise for an individual rider it is most usefully ridden as described below.
- Three or five-metre loops are ridden either side of the centre line. As the centre line is crossed to change the bend, the line taken should be parallel to the short sides.
- Optionally a transition can be ridden as the centre line is crossed.
- At the end of the centre line a small circle of between 6m and 10m is ridden and then the

exercise is repeated back up the centre line, finishing at the point of starting.

AIMS AND BENEFITS

- This exercise is excellent for loosening up horse and rider before more demanding work begins.
- It requires flexibility from both horse and rider while still in the undemanding pace of walk.
- By introducing some halt transitions over the centre line a little more is demanded of the horse's obedience and he is asked to begin to engage his hind legs.
- Using this as an initial exercise, perhaps if the horse is an unknown mount for the rider, it is easy to distinguish the horse's stiff and soft side.

PREPARATION

- The horse should be moving forward with a rhythmical, relaxed walk.
- The rider must look for the centre line and direct the horse into the first loop just beyond the centre line (see diagram).
- As far as possible all loops should be the same size with smooth changes of bend over the centre line.
- If a transition is made the horse should be parallel to the short sides of the arena. He should remain relaxed and calm through the transition.

AIDS AND EXECUTION

- The aids for the loops are: inside leg on the girth for forward movement; outside leg behind the girth for control of the hindquarters; the inside rein asks for the direction; and the outside hand controls the degree of bend in the neck and the speed of the pace.
- A half-halt to prepare the horse for the change-of-direction aids will help keep the change as smooth as possible over the centre line.
- The rider should sit still and maintain a good position so that the horse's balance is not disturbed. The horse can then respond to clear, effective aids positively and fluently.
- If a transition to halt is to be included, again the half-halt preparation becomes imperative, followed by the aids to halt – actively riding the horse from the leg into a closing hand to bring the hind legs under the horse to support him into the halt.
- The halt should be sustained quietly for a second or two or until the rider asks the horse to move forward into the next loop.
- At the end of the centre line a small circle is completed in whichever direction the final loop has designated and then the loop exercise is resumed back up the centre line.
- The number of loops is immaterial but will depend on the size of the arena and the depth of each loop.

RELEVANT TEACHING POINTS

- The instructor should encourage even positioning of the loops and a smooth maintenance of the rhythm.
- Transitions are optional and the instructor may designate when these are to be ridden, giving the rider guidance as to harmony, relaxation and attention of the horse.
- Since the aim of this exercise is to loosen the horse and rider to prepare for further work, emphasis may be placed on not trying too hard and instead thinking about relaxation of horse and rider.

FAULTS

- Transitions to halt may be tense and inconsistent.
- If it is a cold day it may be inappropriate to stay in walk because problems may arise due to horse and/or rider being cold. In this case trot work may be preferable to warm them up more quickly.

MORE DEMANDING LOOPS

Arena
20 x 60m

Gaits
walk, trot and canter

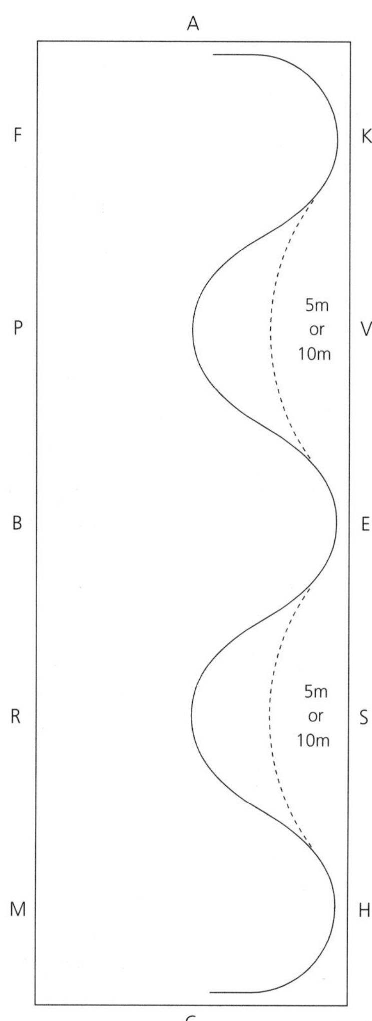

ABOUT THIS EXERCISE

- Here two loops are ridden on the same long side of the arena.
- The first loop leaves the track at the first quarter marker and returns to the track at the half marker.The second loop leaves the track at the half marker and returns to the track at the second quarter marker on the same long side.
- The exercise can and should be ridden on both reins.
- The double loops involve four changes of bend and therefore require greater suppleness from the horse.
- This exercise is easier in a 20m x 60m school.
- The exercise may be ridden in **walk**, **trot** and **canter**. In canter the exercise requires a degree of counter canter and the bend is maintained to the leading leg. **This makes the work in canter more difficult**.
- In **canter** the exercise requires a good degree of balance, suppleness and engagement to enable the horse to move easily from one loop to the next through true canter and a small degree of counter canter on each occasion.

AIMS AND BENEFITS

- To improve the lateral suppleness of the horse.
- To encourage the horse to respond more promptly to the aids for the change of bend.
- To develop equal elasticity of the horse's body.

PREPARATION

- Establish a rhythmical, forward-going gait.
- Ride as good a corner as the horse's balance allows.
- Maintain a good position so that the aid application is clear.
- Make sure that the horse is ready to answer the aids.

AIDS AND EXECUTION

- The inside leg maintains impulsion on the girth.
- The outside leg controls the hindquarters a little behind the girth.
- The inside rein asks for a little direction/flexion.
- The outside rein controls the pace and regulates the degree of flexion.
- The aids are smoothly reversed through each section of the loop where the direction is changed.
- The bend refers to the elasticity throughout the horse's longitudinal axis.
- The bend should be changed smoothly and fluently with no loss of rhythm, balance or harmony.
- In **canter** there is no change of leading leg, and the bend stays with the leading leg.
- The loops should be ridden accurately whilst maintaining rhythm, balance and impulsion.

RELEVANT TEACHING POINTS

- A good corner is essential to enable the two loops to be ridden easily.
- Watching the rider coming towards you is the best way to assess the accuracy of the figures and any faults.
- A smooth change of aids will help ensure a fluently ridden figure.
- Standing at the deepest part of one of the loops often helps the rider gauge the size and shape of the movement.
- The inside aids are always relevant to the direction of the horse's bend; this must never be confused with the inside and outside of the arena.
- Rhythm and balance should be maintained.

FAULTS

- The horse may lose rhythm, balance or impulsion.
- The rider may ride one or other loop too large or irregularly at the expense of the quality of the whole of the movement.
- Stiffness or hollowness, as for the previous exercise, may be apparent, and may even be accentuated in this slightly more difficult movement.

DEVELOPING LOOPS AND CIRCLES

Arena
20 x 40m or
20 x 60m

Gaits
walk, trot and canter

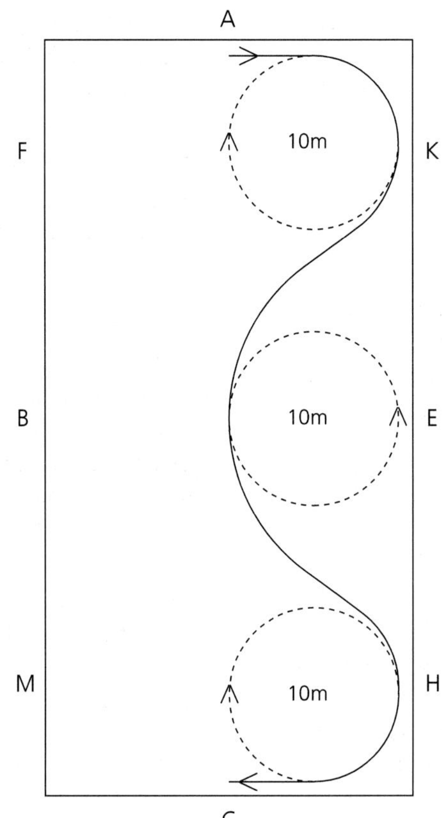

ABOUT THIS EXERCISE

- The exercise starts with one 10m loop on the long side.
- 10m circles are progressively incorporated at the two quarter markers and then at the half marker within the loop.
- Working on the original concept of a change of bend in the 10m loop, the 10m circle at the half marker will be in the opposite direction to the other two circles.
- **Example**: On the right rein commence a 10m loop. Ride a 10m circle at the first quarter marker on the long side. Continue onto the 10m loop and change the bend. Opposite the half marker, i.e. starting and finishing at X , ride a 10m circle to the left. Continue on the loop, change the bend again. Ride a 10m circle at the second quarter marker to finish.
- The exercise may be ridden in **walk**, **trot** and **canter**.
- In **canter** the exercise requires collection – the horse's hind legs sufficiently engaged to maintain balance and impulsion on a small circle. The changes of bend can involve changes of lead through trot or walk (**simple change**); with a more advanced horse **flying changes** may be used.

AIMS AND BENEFITS

- To improve the suppleness and obedience of the horse.
- By developing smaller circles, to encourage greater engagement of the hind legs and lateral bend.

- To improve the horse's ability to work in self-carriage (e.g. the hind legs carrying more weight and the forehand therefore being lighter, with the horse in balance).

PREPARATION

- The horse must be forward and obedient.
- A well ridden corner is essential.
- **Simple changes** (transitions through walk) require engagement and balance.
- **Flying changes** need a well-balanced, energetic canter and a clear understanding of the aids for the change.

AIDS AND EXECUTION

- It is preferable in trot that the work is ridden sitting.
- Inside leg on the girth maintains impulsion. Outside leg a little behind the girth controls the hindquarters.
- The inside rein guides direction; outside rein controls the pace and the degree of flexion through the neck.
- The aids are smoothly reversed through each phase of the exercise and each change of direction.
- Rhythm, forwardness, bend through the horse's body with even smooth changes of direction are desired criteria for the exercise.

RELEVANT TEACHING POINTS

- The exercise develops preparation, coordination and accuracy.
- An excellent progressively developed exercise for groups or individuals.
- The exercise can be used for class lessons and adds an element of fun because riders really need to keep their distance and think.
- By concentrating the rider's mind on the figures, often the horse's rhythm and balance improve radically. This can be the result of the rider concentrating hard on something else. The exercise itself then improves the quality of work.
- The ride should be worked in open order and be well spaced; each rider should commence a phase of the movement at the same time. Up to six riders is manageable; eight is possible but only with a more skilled teacher.
- Progression of the exercise is simple as long as each rider maintains a well-regulated space between himself and the rider in front.

FAULTS

- The horse may change the rhythm or lose impulsion.
- There may be a lack of bend, especially on the stiff side.
- Stiffness may cause a loss of accuracy and quality of the movement.
- The rider may lose the plan of the movement and cause a collision with other riders.
- In canter the horse may lose balance and change legs.
- In canter the horse may fall onto his forehand, and the length of stride and balance will suffer.

MORE SMALL CIRCLES

Arena
20 x 40m or
20 x 60m

Gaits
walk, trot and canter

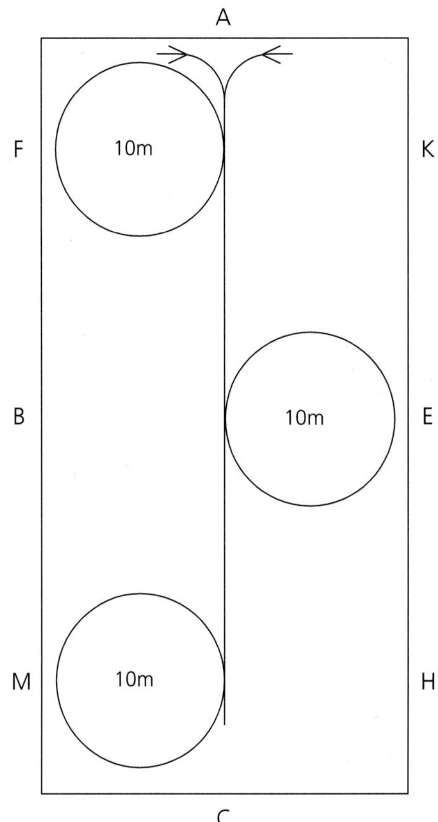

ABOUT THIS EXERCISE

- 10m circles can be ridden from the centre line to the wall or vice versa.
- If ridden from the centre line, the exercise first requires a turn onto the centre line and then a series of 10m circles can be made either side of the centre line.
- Three circles can be fitted into a 20 x 40m arena, but working in a large (20 x 60m) arena affords more space.
- The circles can be ridden on turns at A or C from both directions.
- The exercise can be ridden by individuals or groups of riders.
- This type of movement is sometimes found in dressage tests of Elementary standard.
- The exercise can be ridden in **walk**, **trot** or **canter**.
- In **canter**, the exercise requires a greater degree of balance and engagement. The changes of direction can be ridden as changes of lead through trot or walk (**simple changes**) or as **flying changes**.

AIMS AND BENEFITS

- Well-ridden circles improve suppleness, obedience and balance of the horse.
- Develops greater engagement of the hind legs and helps improve lateral bend.
- Encourages better self-carriage by bringing weight off the forehand.

PREPARATION

- The exercise would most usefully be ridden in walk and trot. However, it is probably easier to ride the circles in sitting trot. Canter is possible but requires a more advanced horse who shows good balance, engagement and self-carriage.
- A well-ridden turn onto the centre line is essential.
- The rider must keep control of the outside shoulder and hindquarters through the turn, so that the horse is straight before riding the first circle.
- The horse must be forward and on the aids.

AIDS AND EXECUTION

- The inside leg on the girth maintains impulsion, particularly keeping the horse active through his inside hind leg.
- The outside leg controls the hindquarters, a little behind the girth.
- The inside rein creates the bend and direction.
- The outside rein controls the amount of bend and the pace.

RELEVANT TEACHING POINTS

- As the horse is asked to work more on the smaller circles, he may try to evade more (see Faults).
- The instructor's position is all-important if he is to see the way the exercise is ridden and to offer appropriate help.
- Stand towards the A–C line but just off centre.
- Observe the centre line carefully.
- If working with a group, the riders should be in open order and each rider should be in a different part of the exercise at the same time.
- Turns away after the exercise could be alternatively to left and to right.
- Make riders aware that if a horse is progressing back up the long side to recommence the exercise, they may need to ride a 9m circle (just off the outside track) to allow horses to pass each other safely.
- Awareness increases competence and prepares riders for working-in situations at competitions.

FAULTS

- The horse may lose impulsion (activity of the hind legs) on the small circle.
- The horse may lose rhythm and bend.
- The hindquarters may escape on the turn onto the centre line or in any of the circles.
- The horse may be crooked on the centre line (hindquarters escaping, hind legs not following the same line as the front legs).
- The circles may be too large or irregular in shape.

20M CIRCLE AND TRANSITIONS

Arena
20 x 40m or
20 x 60m

Gaits
walk, trot and canter

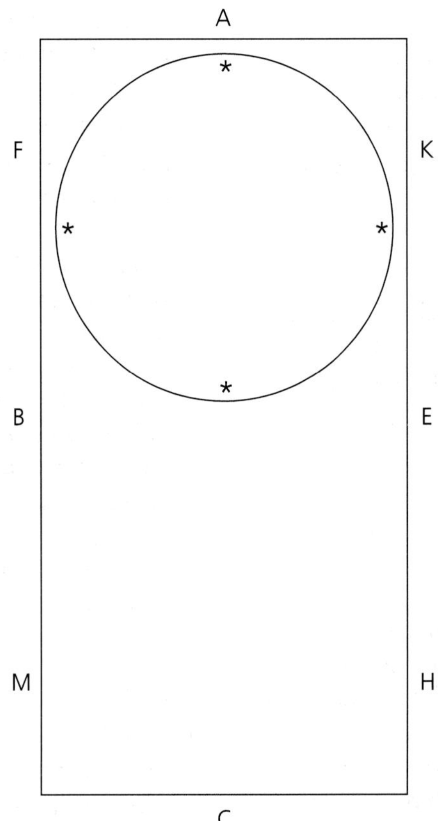

ABOUT THIS EXERCISE

- The 20m circle can be ridden at either end of the school or in the centre of the school at E or B.
- Transitions can be ridden at one or more points around the circle.
- As the exercise progresses a maximum of four transitions can be ridden to good effect on one circle.
- This exercise can usefully be ridden in **walk**, **trot** and **canter**.
- The transitions can be progressive (e.g. walk to trot, or canter to trot) or direct (e.g.walk to canter or trot to halt).
- Progressive transitions are easier for less-experienced riders and more novice horses.
- Direct transitions test the skill of a more experienced rider and demand more engagement from the more educated horse.
- The transitions should be ridden smoothly, aiming for the horse to move evenly from a clear stride of one pace, to a clear stride of the new pace.
- The transition can involve many steps in the new pace, or as few as two or three steps before returning to the original pace again. The latter will make greater demands on the horse's obedience, balance and coordination.
- The exercise can be ridden by an individual or a group of up to four riders on one circle, riding the transitions in open order.

AIMS AND BENEFITS

- Circles improve lateral suppleness.
- Transitions improve engagement of the hindquarters, balance and self-carriage.
- Transitions improve response to the aids and suppleness of the horse's back.

PREPARATION

- Rhythm and impulsion on a well-shaped circle will prepare the horse for a balanced transition.
- If the rider thinks ahead he will be better prepared to apply the aids smoothly.

AIDS AND EXECUTION

- If making transitions from trot to walk, it is probably preferable to ride the circle in sitting trot.
- In riding the transition, a preparatory half-halt (warning the horse of the aid to follow) should be applied just before the aid for the change of pace.
- Maintaining a secure but supple position, both legs are applied to engage the hind legs under the horse. The closing of both hands signifies to the horse a transfer to a lower pace.
- As the change of pace is felt, the rider must allow the horse to travel fluently into the new gait.

RELEVANT TEACHING POINTS

- Emphasis on the value of transitions can never be too great.
- Transitions are probably the single most valuable tool in training the horse.
- In helping the rider to ride better transitions, **preparation** is all-important.
- Help the rider to be more aware of the feel of the horse and therefore the timing of the transition.
- Preparation and correct, clear aid application with good timing will lead to harmonious transitions.
- Set up the first two transitions on opposite sides of the circles (e.g. X and A). Then incorporate the third and fourth transitions to make the exercise more demanding.
- In **canter**, the pace will require further balance and engagement, especially if acute transitions (e.g. walk to canter or canter to walk) are attempted.

FAULTS

- If the transitions lack preparation, the horse may lose harmony through the change of pace.
- This may be seen in resistance from the horse, hollowing his back and/or coming above the bit.
- The horse must not be allowed to 'slow down' into the transition., reducing activity in the hind legs rather than stepping more powerfully under with the hind legs.
- The horse must not evade the engagement by losing straightness (e.g. falling out through the shoulder or swinging the quarters in).

CIRCLES LARGE AND SMALL

Arena
20 x 40m or
20 x 60m

Gaits
walk, trot
and canter

—*— = tangent
point of circle

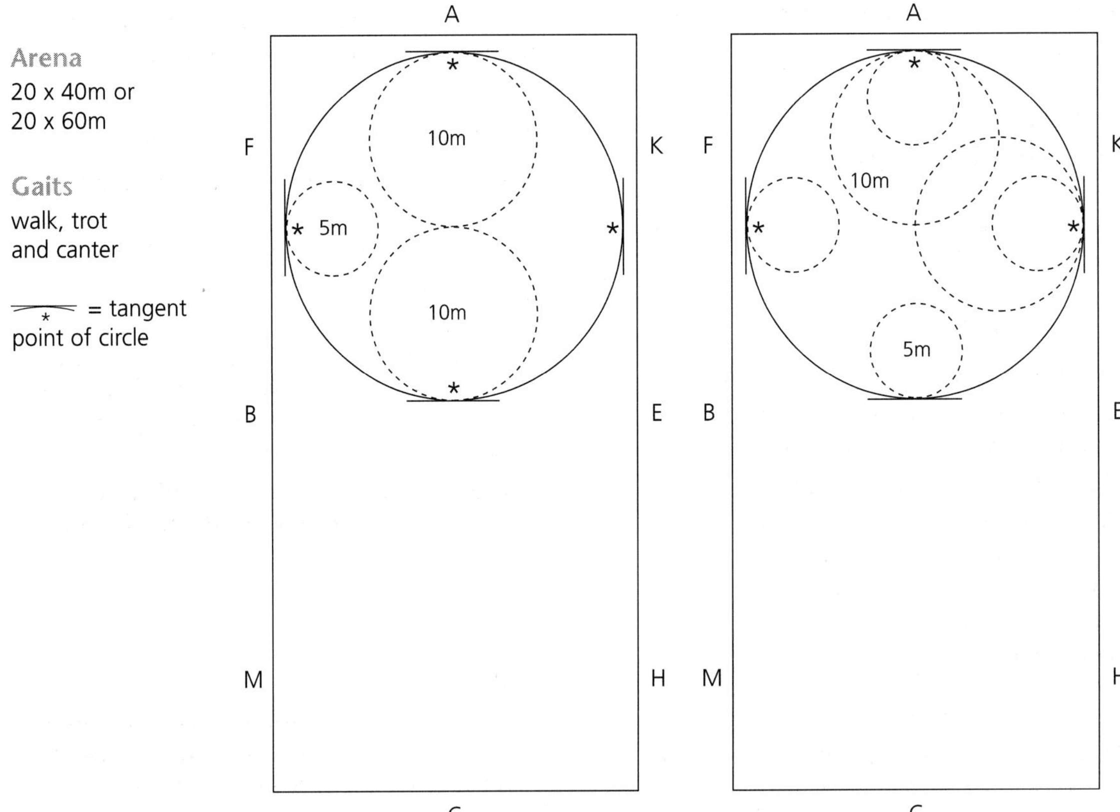

ABOUT THIS EXERCISE

- The 20m circle can be ridden at A,C,E,or B.
- Small circles are then added progressively at one or more tangent points of the circle.
- The small circles can be 5m or 10m, depending on the pace at which they are ridden.
- 5m circles should be ridden in **walk**.
- 10m circles could be ridden in **trot** and **canter**.
- As the exercise develops, more small circles can be included.
- The exercise can be usefully ridden in one specific pace or in a combination of **walk**, **trot** and **canter**, with the transitions being progressive or direct.
- Variation of pace will add interest to horse and rider and keep the horse more attentive to the aids.
- If ridden in **canter** the exercise is **more demanding** for the horse, requiring better engagement and balance, particularly on the smaller circles.
- The exercise can be ridden individually or in groups of up to four riders.
- Group-riding of this exercise requires concentration, accuracy, good preparation and awareness of other riders.

AIMS AND BENEFITS

- Improve suppleness, balance and co-ordination.
- Improve response and obedience to the aids.

- Small circles improve engagement and self-carriage.

PREPARATION

- Circles should be well planned and accurately ridden.
- The second half of the circle should be ridden to match the first half.

AIDS AND EXECUTION

- Commence a 20m circle in the chosen pace.
- At one tangent point make a transition to walk and commence a 5m circle in walk.
- Finish the 5m circle and make a transition into trot to continue on the 20m circle.
- Any choice of pace and variation can be made to suit the level of competence of horse and/or rider. For example, in trot, ride the 20m circle, take a 10m circle at one tangent point of the circle maintaining the same pace and then return to the 20m circle still in trot.
- Inside leg on the girth (maintaining impulsion), outside leg behind the girth (controlling the hindquarters), inside rein (asking for direction), outside rein (controlling pace and degree of flexion in the neck).
- Apply the aids smoothly and in harmony with the horse to create a fluent movement.

RELEVANT TEACHING POINTS

- Help the rider to be aware of good rhythm and balance.
- Encourage understanding of too much bend in the neck and losing straightness.
- The instructor should be positioned a little to the outside of the circle so that it is easy to see the rider(s) and offer them assistance, but not be in their way when they are negotiating smaller circles within the 20m circle.
- **Encourage the rider to test the self-carriage of the horse in canter by surrendering the reins for two or three strides.**

FAULTS

- Poor-shaped circles.
- The horse's hind legs must not slow down, they must step in a more lively way under the horse's body particularly on the smaller circles.
- Check the horse's straightness, especially as the circles become smaller and ask more of the horse.

SATELLITE CIRCLES

Arena
20 x 40m or
20 x 60m

Gaits
walk, trot and canter

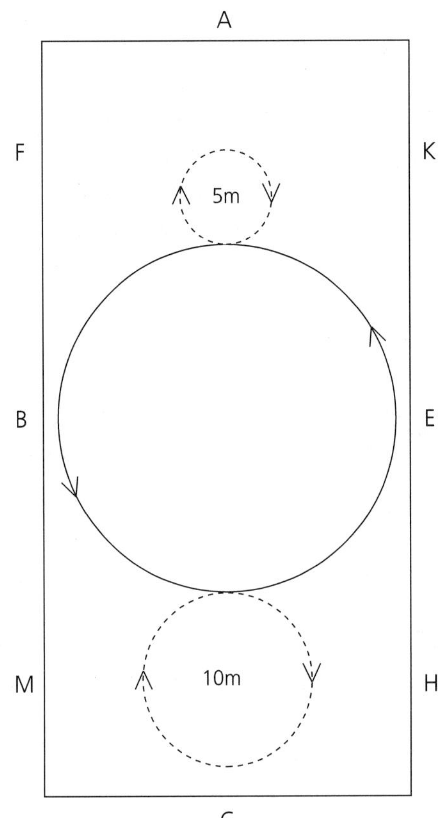

ABOUT THIS EXERCISE

- The exercise is built up on a 20m circle centred on the middle of the school from E or B.
- The same basic principles apply as for the previous exercise. The main difference is that the small circles are ridden in the opposite direction to the main 20m circle.
- The small circle is ridden as a 'satellite' off the large circle.
- The main circle can be ridden on both reins in **walk**, **trot** and **canter**.
- The satellite circles (one or two) are ridden by changing the direction at the appropriate point and then returning to the main circle by changing the direction again.
- The satellite circles can be ridden in **walk**, **trot** or **canter**.
- In **canter** the exercise demands greater ability from both horse and rider. The satellite circles require a change of leading leg either through trot or walk (a simple change) or through canter (flying change).

AIMS AND BENEFITS

- To further develop the obedience and suppleness of the horse.
- To further develop the competence and effectiveness of the rider.
- To give riders more scope in the work they use to develop the horse's training.

- To encourage greater lateral suppleness, engagement of the hind legs, balance and self-carriage.
- To develop the horse's versatility.
- To further develop rhythm and maintenance of forward movement through changes of direction.

PREPARATION

- Choose the pace and establish a rhythmical, forward-going gait.
- Think ahead and ride the basic 20m circle with care, maintaining rhythm, bend, forward movement and straightness.
- Make sure that the horse is 'in front of the leg' and listening to the aids before commencing the first change of direction into the 'satellite' circle.

AIDS AND EXECUTION

- If using trot, it would be advisable to ride the small circles in sitting trot.
- The aids for the circle are as in previous exercises.
- The change of bend must be well prepared and ridden fluently.
- Be aware that through the change of bend the horse may be more likely to lose balance, impulsion and forward movement.
- Moving from a larger to a smaller circle, requires a greater degree of activity of the hind leg and more bend through the body for the smaller circle.
- On returning to the large circle the horse should feel in better balance and self-carriage as a result of the effect of the small circle.

RELEVANT TEACHING POINTS

- The horse may find the small circles easier on the soft or hollow side and appear more reluctant to bend on the stiff side.
- The rider must be aware of how to ride more positively with the inside leg on the stiff side, to generate an active inside hind leg to help the horse become more supple.
- Similarly the rider must be made aware of the need to control the degree of flexion with greater care on the soft or hollow side so that the horse does not lose his weight through the outside shoulder and so lose straightness.
- The instructor can usefully stand in the middle of the main 20m circle, which will not impede the riding of the satellite circles.
- In this position it is easy to observe the change of bend from one circle to the other and to watch the horse's reaction, and the rider's position and aid application.

FAULTS

- Many of the faults listed under the previous exercises apply here.
- Loss of rhythm, balance or forward movement.
- Falling in (lack of activity of the inside hind leg) on the stiff side and falling out through the shoulder (too much neck bend) on the hollow side.
- Poor-shaped circles – because it is harder to judge the size and shape of circles with no walls to support.

CONCENTRIC CIRCLES

Arena
20 x 40m or
20 x 60m

Gaits
walk, trot and canter

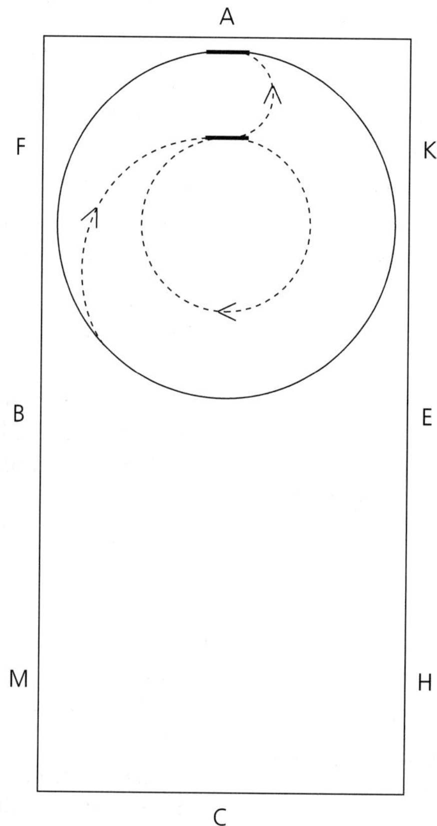

ABOUT THIS EXERCISE

- The basis of the exercise is a 20m circle, which can be ridden anywhere in the school, but is probably easiest to establish at A or C.
- The exercise can be ridden in **walk**, **trot** (sitting on the smaller circle) or **canter** or in any combination of these paces.
- The pace is established with a good rhythm and impulsion.
- The circle is reduced in size to around 10m.
- The pace is then reduced (e.g. trot to walk, or canter to trot).
- A small half circle is then ridden from the reduced circle back onto the original 20m circle to proceed in the opposite direction.
- On reaching the 20m circle again, the pace is then increased (e.g. trot back to canter, or walk back to trot or canter).
- The exercise can be ridden individually or in groups.
- With groups of riders (up to four on one circle) the exercise demands concentration, good preparation, accuracy of aid application and awareness of other riders.

AIMS AND BENEFITS

- To develop versatility of horse and rider.
- To further develop suppleness and obedience.
- To improve response to transitions and therefore engagement of the hind legs.

- Through better engagement to improve balance and self-carriage.
- To increase the knowledge and scope of the rider's range of exercises from which the horse can be further worked and improved.
- If ridden in **canter**, as described below, the exercise encourages good engagement and better self-carriage. The effects of the exercise can be clearly felt.

PREPARATION

- Establish rhythm and forwardness in the initial gait.
- Establish a carefully ridden 20m circle.
- Make sure that the horse is listening and on the aids.

AIDS AND EXECUTION

- The aids for riding the circle are as previously described on page 19.
- Progressively decrease the circle while maintaining the rhythm, forward movement and helping the horse to maintain balance as the smaller circle makes him work harder.
- On 10m maintain activity and ride a well-prepared downward transition (e.g. from trot to walk).
- Change the aids (e.g. from left to right) and ride a small half circle outwards to rejoin the 20m circle going on the opposite rein.
- Make an upward transition in the new direction.
- This exercise is extremely effective if ridden as follows: In trot on a 20m circle (e.g. to the left) decrease the circle progressively to 10m. Make a well-prepared transition to walk on the 10m circle. Change the bend to the right and at the same time make a small half circle outwards in walk to join the 20m circle on the right rein. Apply the aids for right canter and make a transition directly to canter from walk. Proceed in canter on the circle.
- **If building up the exercise in canter:** canter the 20m circle, decrease the canter, make a direct transition to walk, ride a half circle out and then move directly up into canter on the new rein.

RELEVANT TEACHING POINTS

- Sufficient energy must be maintained, particularly when the circle is reduced in size.
- The instructor needs to stand to the outside of the circle so that the riders are not impeded.
- If two circles are working simultaneously at both ends of the school, which is perfectly practical, the instructor could position himself/herself at E or B and have ample view of both groups of riders.
- The rider(s) must be encouraged not to rush the transitions, particularly if direct transitions are being asked for.
- The rider(s) must be encouraged to believe that the exercise will encourage greater activity from the horse and so the transition will be easy for him.
- Anxiety, anticipation or a change in body position of the rider in an effort to effect the transition will usually be detrimental to the result.
- This is an exercise that teaches the rider to prepare, give clear aids and then wait for the result.

FAULTS

- The impulsion and rhythm may be lost as the circle decreases and this will adversely affect the following transition.
- The rider may hurry the horse in anxiety to achieve the upward transition after the half circle.
- Rushed or ill-prepared aid application may cause a loss of balance and harmony.
- As in previous circle exercises, the problems of stiffness on one side and hollowness on the other side may be apparent.

SHORTENING AND LENGTHENING ON CIRCLES

Arena
20 x 40m or
20 x 60m

Gaits
trot or canter

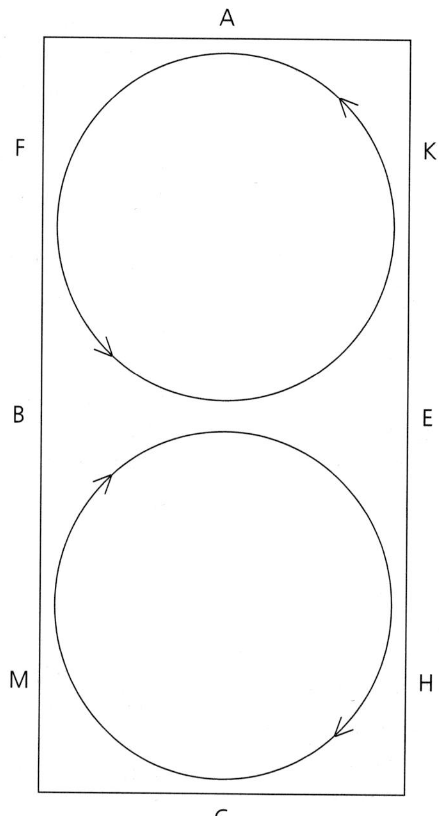

ABOUT THIS EXERCISE

- This exercise can be ridden in **trot** or **canter**.
- In **canter** the horse needs to be a little fitter and more balanced to benefit fully from the exercise.
- The exercise can be ridden individually or in groups of riders working in open order.
- The gait is established with good rhythm, balance and forward movement.
- If working in groups an even number of riders establish a 20m circle at each end of the school.
- On each circle the riders are encouraged to shorten and lengthen the stride, either a few steps at a time, or possibly on half the circle alternately: e.g. half circle from C to X, collect the steps, making the horse livelier, rounder and with greater athleticism in his back, shoulders and neck; on the second half of the circle, open the steps and encourage the horse to take bigger strides from active hind legs, slightly lengthening the horse's frame.
- In a 20 x 60m school the circles can be ridden on the same rein as there is plenty of room between the two circles for the horses to pass comfortably. In a 20 x 40m school, however, it is wiser and safer to have one circle on the right rein and one circle on the left rein. In this position horses do not meet each other head-on, which may upset them; instead they meet travelling in the same direction (see diagram).
- This exercise can be comfortably ridden with up to eight riders (four at each end).

AIMS AND BENEFITS

- The circles help to supple the horse, particularly when worked on both reins.
- The changes of direction add variety.
- The shortening and lengthening helps to engage the horse and develop more scope in his paces.
- Keeps horse and rider interested in their work.

PREPARATION

- Two circles are established one at either end of the school.
- The rhythm must be secure and the horse must be going forward with a positive attitude.

AIDS AND EXECUTION

- The inside leg maintains impulsion on the girth.
- The outside leg controls the hindquarters from a position a little behind the girth.
- The inside rein creates direction for the circle.
- The outside rein controls the speed of the pace and also the degree of bend through the neck.
- From a good rhythmical trot the horse is asked to engage the hind legs more underneath him and contain his frame into a rounder more elevated shape (the shoulders lift, the back appears stronger and more supple and the horse comes up through the wither).
- This shorter, rounder trot is achieved with a series of half-halts to encourage the horse to carry himself with the weight off his forehand.
- It is essential that the rider is aware of the importance of the hind legs becoming more active with supple use of the joints.
- The horse must **never** slow down in his more collected work. The hind legs **must** stay lively which in turn will keep progressing the development of self-carriage.

RELEVANT TEACHING POINTS

- The instructor is best positioned to see the horses on both circles by standing a little off the track between the E and B line. From this position he can effectively watch both circles at the same time.
- There must be emphasis on encouraging the pupils to be aware of the feel of active hind legs.
- There must be awareness of when the horse tries to 'slow down' rather than step more actively through with the hind legs.
- The rider should be looking for only a few strides of bigger trot, then a few strides of smaller trot – it is the transitions which are most valuable, encouraging the horse to listen and respond and therefore engage the quarters more and develop self-carriage.
- In a 20 x 40m school there is the possibility of riders being intimidated by the proximity of other riders.
- Always mount riders well within their level of scope and their ability to improve; they should then not be over-horsed, which can lead to anxiety and further problems.
- The riders must change the rein frequently so that they work on both reins and learn to be aware of when to change the rein to keep the balance of numbers of riders correct on each circle.

FAULTS

- The circle is not ridden with sufficient accuracy and attention to detail.
- The rhythm may be variable; the straightness may be a problem.
- The horse may hollow and not sustain his forwardness without a struggle.
- The rider may allow the horse to hurry rather than be aware of the need to keep the same tempo (speed of the pace – mph).
- The rider may lose activity of the hind legs, as the horse slows down and does not step more through.
- The rider may ask for too many strides in the new (shortened or lengthened) pace.

USING SHORT DIAGONAL LINES

Arena
20 x 40m or
20 x 60m

Gaits
trot/walk

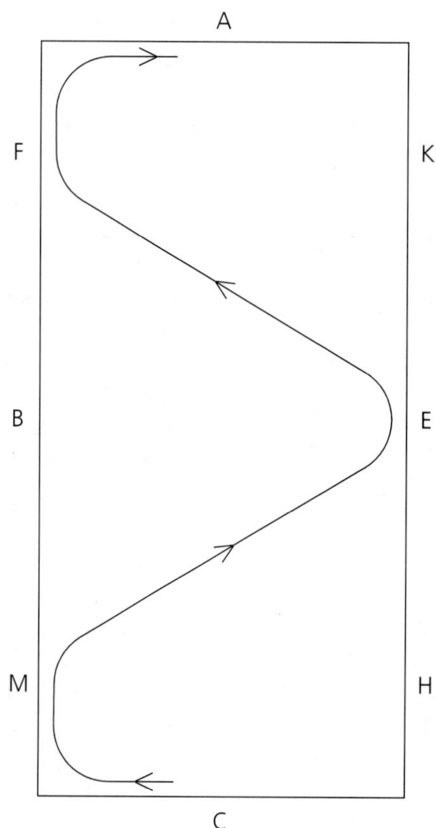

ABOUT THIS EXERCISE

- This exercise can be ridden in a 20 x 40m or 20 x 60m school. It is easier in the latter because there is more space.
- It is most usefully ridden in **trot** and can be used for individuals or groups. In group sessions this exercise can be performed in closed or open order.
- The exercise is ridden from the first quarter marker after the short side, across the school to the half marker on the opposite side, then a change of direction is made to take the line back to the quarter marker at the end of the first long side. The rider ends the exercise by going large on the same rein he started on.
- The exercise could be ridden in **walk** to practise the lines and ground pattern, and also for less competent riders to give them time to execute the changes of direction.

AIMS AND BENEFITS

- This exercise develops the flexibility of the horse by accustoming him to frequent changes of direction.
- It therefore improves his suppleness and response to the aids.
- Similarly it improves the rider's co-ordination and timing of aid application.
- The exercise improves the rider's versatility in the use of the school.

- As a group exercise ridden in closed order, it improves the rider's control and forward thinking.

PREPARATION

- The exercise may first be ridden in walk to help the rider to be familiar with the floor plan of the movement, or if the horse is young and green.
- Begin by riding in a good rhythm in either walk or trot, going large around the arena.
- Make sure that the horse is listening to the rider and in front of the leg.
- The rider maintains a good position so that the aids can be clearly applied and chooses from which quarter marker the exercise will commence.

AIDS AND EXECUTION

- The horse is directed off the track at the quarter marker by applying the inside leg on the girth to maintain impulsion, meanwhile the outside leg guards the quarters making sure they follow the forehand 'straight'.
- The inside rein directs the horse onto the short diagonal line, and at the same time the outside rein controls the degree of direction and the speed of the pace.
- The horse is ridden forward in rhythm on the short diagonal line.
- As the half marker is approached the rider applies one or more half-halts to balance the horse and warn him that another aid is to be given.
- The direction is changed and the aids applied (as described) to direct the horse on the new line to the second quarter marker.
- On completing the two diagonal lines, the horse is ridden large around the arena.

RELEVANT TEACHING POINTS

- The rhythm and activity in the pace must be maintained throughout the exercise.
- The change of direction aids must be smoothly applied to enable the horse to move through the exercise harmoniously and with balance and confidence.
- The exercise should be ridden from both directions equally.

FAULTS

- The horse may lose rhythm and/or impulsion through the changes of direction.
- The horse may fall in on his stiff side and produce too much bend in the neck on his hollow side, so losing the weight through his outside shoulder.
- In both cases the instructor should help the rider to counteract the relevant fault with greater support from the appropriate leg or rein aid or a combination of the two.
- The horse will probably find the exercise easier in one direction than the other. The weaker direction should be worked on to try to make the work more even.

DEVELOPING THE SHORT DIAGONAL EXERCISE

Arena
20 x 40m
or
20 x 60m

Gaits
trot/walk

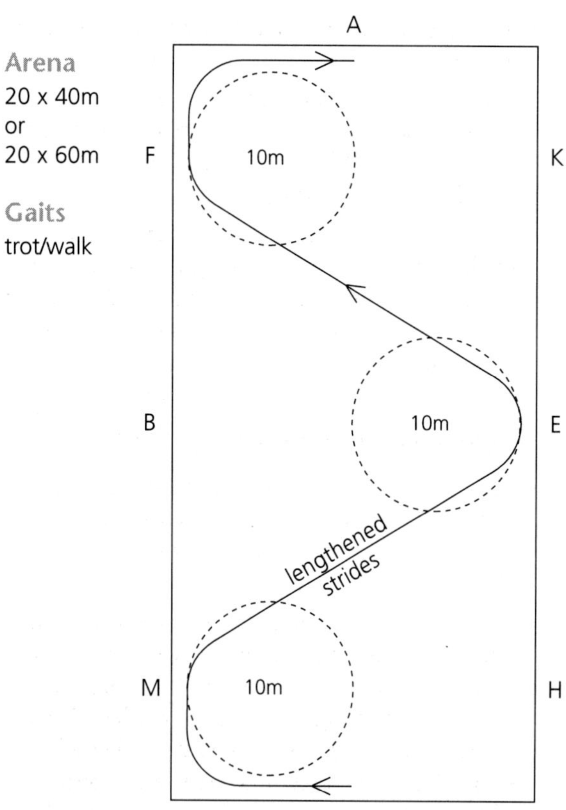

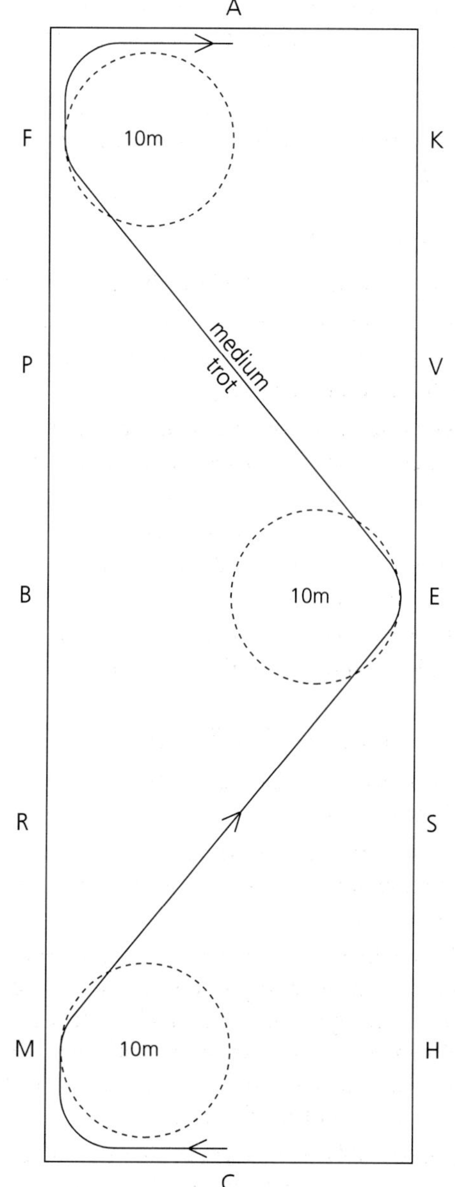

ABOUT THIS EXERCISE

- This exercise repeats the basic floor plan of the previous exercise but includes a 10m circle at the two quarter markers at the start and end of the exercise.
- The work is most beneficial in **trot** but the exercise can be ridden in walk just to give the rider an idea of where the movements are ridden.
- Optionally a third 10m circle can be added at the half marker.
- Optionally the short diagonal lines may be ridden in working trot, showing a few lengthened strides, or medium trot.
- Can be ridden individually, or in a group working in open order.

AIMS AND BENEFITS

- Continuing from the previous exercise the difficulty is increased to make greater demands on the horse's suppleness and responsiveness.
- Similarly, the rider will be further taxed in aid preparation and co-ordination.

- Changing the length of stride within the pace requires a further degree of flexibility from the horse.
- The 10m circles will help increase the engagement of the hind legs towards improved collection.

PREPARATION

- The preparation for the basic floor plan applies.
- Before the first quarter marker a half-halt will be made to make sure that the horse is active and in front of the rider's leg.
- The horse is ridden onto a 10m circle and from this circle the short diagonal line is ridden.
- If a second circle is to be ridden at the half marker then one or more half-halts will alert the horse to the change of direction and the following circle aids.
- The second short diagonal is ridden and preparation made for the next 10m circle.

AIDS AND EXECUTION

- The aids as described apply to the overall riding of the exercise.
- Half-halt preparation sets the horse onto his hocks around the corner prior to the first part of the exercise.
- The circles are ridden with the inside leg on the girth to maintain impulsion, and the outside leg behind the girth to control and guard the hindquarters; meanwhile the inside rein directs the movement and the outside rein controls the bend and regulates the pace.
- It is probably preferable for the rider to be in sitting trot, as the horse should be supple enough to maintain softness and balance. In sitting trot the rider should be better able to apply effective, co-ordinated aids.
- When asking for lengthened strides on one or both of the short diagonal lines, the energy should be asked for gradually while keeping the horse balanced and not allowing him to quicken the pace.
- After a few longer strides then, similarly, the horse should be asked to compress his steps by using tactful half-halts to bring him into rounder, higher steps again.
- If asking for medium trot, the transition from working trot to medium trot and back should be quite defined; whereas if showing lengthened strides, the transition to and from will be more progressive.

RELEVANT TEACHING POINTS

- Care must be taken to ride the figure accurately, as this will require greater obedience and therefore suppleness from the horse and also effectiveness and co-ordination from the rider.
- When developing the range of stride within the pace it is important that the rider is aware of the difference between the horse lengthening his stride and hurrying. When the horse lengthens he covers more ground with each stride and moves from one point to another faster **because** of the longer stride. When the horse hurries he travels quicker (in ground speed) from marker to marker but not because the stride is bigger. In fact often as the horse hurries the strides become shorter as the weight comes off the hind legs and he runs onto his forehand.

FAULTS

- Rhythm or impulsion may be lost, particularly on the small circles, if the horse does not stay actively in front of the rider's leg.
- The horse may show stiffness in one direction and hollowness in the other so that straightness is affected.
- The horse may hurry and run onto his forehand when asked for bigger steps rather than stay on his hocks and lengthen the stride from active hind legs.

IMPROVING CORNERS WITH HALT TRANSITIONS

Arena
20 x 40m or
20 x 60m

Gaits
walk, trot and canter

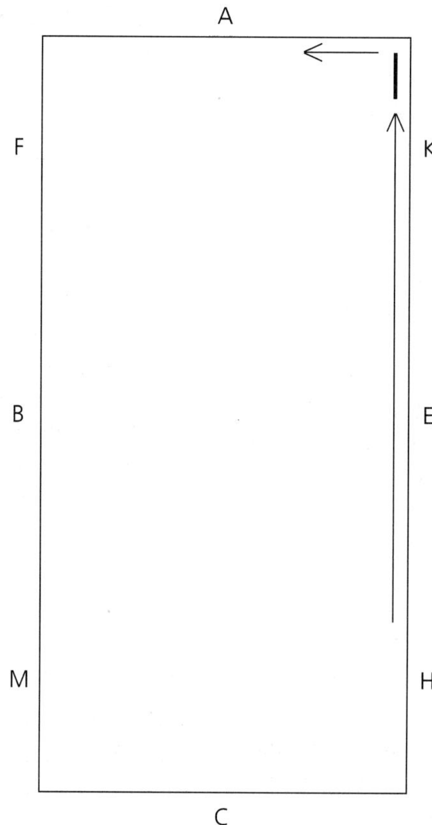

ABOUT THIS EXERCISE

- This exercise involves riding down the side of the school (short or long side) and making a transition in the corner before allowing the horse to turn to the new side.
- The horse is required to wait in the transition before being asked to move off again.
- The transitions can be ridden from a basic pace of **walk**, **trot** or **canter**.
- The exercise could be introduced in **walk**, to **halt**, and then on to **trot.**
- The most effective use of the exercise is to ride from **trot** to **halt** and back to **trot** again; however the transitions can be progressive, i.e. from trot through walk to halt and progressively upwards to trot.
- Transitions can be made in each of the four corners or they can be ridden selectively in one or more of the corners.
- The exercise could be ridden in **canter** to either **trot** or **halt**. This requires greater engagement and balance from the horse.
- The exercise can be ridden by individuals or in groups. In groups the work should be carried out with the riders in open order.

AIMS AND BENEFITS

- To improve the riding of corners – essential whether schooling or riding a dressage test.
- This exercise improves the engagement of the horse's inside hind leg, so developing his balance and self-carriage.

- The exercise helps to prevent the natural tendency for the horse to anticipate the corner and start to move automatically through it, taking his weight onto the inside shoulder, without waiting for the rider's aids to tell him to make the turn.
- By insisting that the horse stays straight and accepts a transition in the corner, the rider is reaffirming the need for the horse to remain attentive to the rider and not anticipate an obvious turn.
- With the rider choosing the corners where the transitions will be made and not necessarily riding a transition in every corner, the horse will need to stay obedient to the rider's aids.
- The transition, or the anticipation of possibly being asked to make one, will encourage the horse to keep his weight on his hind legs and, particularly, stay active through the inside hind leg. In this way he will not fall onto his shoulders through the corners, loading the forehand.
- Due to the position of the horse (facing the wall) he will automatically turn with little indication from the rider, as there is nowhere else for him to go, so the rider can be aware of the motivation of the hind legs and the horse picking up his shoulders to move into the turn.

PREPARATION

- The horse must be ridden forward with energy and rhythm.
- The horse should be straight on the long or short side (hind legs tracking the forelegs).

AIDS AND EXECUTION

- A half-halt is made to warn and prepare the horse of the impending transition.
- The inside leg is active on the girth to maintain energy but prevent the horse from falling onto the inside shoulder.
- The outside leg controls the hindquarters.
- The inside hand maintains a light, allowing feel through the rein.
- The outside hand keeps the horse straight and prevents him from beginning to anticipate the turn of his own accord.
- The inside leg may need to be more lively than normal into the corner, to prevent the horse from lying against the leg to evade working through the corner.
- The horse must be rewarded for the transition (a pat on the neck or quietly spoken 'good boy') and he must be encouraged to stay still for as long as the rider wishes before inviting him to move off into the turn.
- In the move-off, the legs should predominate, allowing the wall to turn the horse with minimal direction aid from the rein.
- The horse should be asked to move off from the transition with lively activity.

RELEVANT TEACHING POINTS

- The rider must be encouraged to feel whether the horse is straight before the transition.
- The rider must be encouraged to feel the natural tendency for the horse to offer the corner without really waiting for the rider's aids. With this feel in mind, the rider can then learn when and how actively to use the inside leg.
- The transitions should be worked evenly on both reins.

FAULTS

- The horse may try to anticipate the corner, beginning to make the turn before the rider actually asks for the turn.
- The horse may be a little anxious in the halt transition, being reluctant to stand still quietly, awaiting the next aid.
- Tension, as a result of the influence of the transitions, may cause a loss of rhythm or an increase in tempo (speed) of the pace.
- As in previous exercises the horse may show stiffness on one rein and hollowness on the other.

HALTS WITH TURN ON THE FOREHAND

Arena
20 x 40m or
20m 60m

Gaits
walk, trot and canter

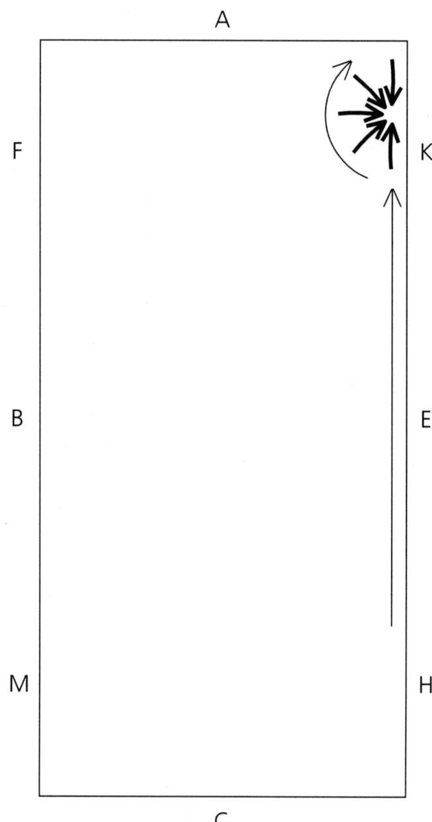

ABOUT THIS EXERCISE

- This exercise is a development from the previous one. Here, instead of continuing on the same rein from the halt transition in the corner, a turn on the forehand through 180° is executed and horse and rider proceed on the opposite rein along the same line as the approach.
- The rider moves forward straight into the halt as previously described, say, on the left rein, then from the halt a turn on the forehand to the right is made and the horse proceeds forward on the right rein.
- Can be ridden in **walk**, **trot** or **canter**.

AIMS AND BENEFITS

- Turn on the forehand can be useful in helping the rider to develop co-ordination of the aids.
- It helps give the rider feel for the horse moving other than just forward.
- Using this exercise as a variation on the previous one will will assist in preventing the horse from anticipating the move-off forward from the halt. and help keep him attentive to the aids.
- Turn on the forehand improves the responsiveness of the horse to the aids and encourages him to think about moving in a lateral direction as well as forwards.
- While some trainers argue that a turn on the forehand does not encourage carrying power of the hind legs, the benefits from increasing responsiveness to the aids should not be ignored.

PREPARATION

- The exercise can be ridden from **walk** (to halt) or from **trot** (to halt). If the turn is ridden from **walk** it is then known as a turn about the forehand. In this case the inside foreleg does not pivot in the turn and the horse maintains the rhythm in the walk without coming to a full stop.
- The horse should be ridden purposefully forward with a good rhythm and impulsion.
- The rider should be aware of the straightness and ride a half-halt in preparation for the halt transition.
- The rider must be clear about the aids for the movement.

AIDS AND EXECUTION

- The horse is ridden forward to an active halt as described in the last exercise.
- The horse is facing the wall, parallel to one side of the school.
- The aids are applied as follows to effect a turn on the forehand.
- From halt, the inside leg moves a little behind the girth to encourage the horse to move away in a step-by-step movement.
- The rider's outside leg, as usual a little behind the girth, controls the quarters and regulates the speed and size of the sideways steps.
- The inside rein maintains a hint of flexion through the gullet (the horse is almost straight).
- The outside rein controls the degree of bend in the neck and prevents the horse from moving forward.
- The horse's hind legs move on a large semi-circle around the forelegs; the horse makes the turn within his own length.
- The horse should not travel forward in the movement but he **must** not move backward.
- The horse should be encouraged to move actively forward after the turn to re-establish a rhythmical, lively pace.

RELEVANT TEACHING POINTS

- It is easy for a less experienced rider to be confused about 'inside' and 'outside' with reference to the bend of the horse. This must be emphasised until it is clear.
- If necessary, it may help to give the rider a demonstration of the movement.
- It is sometimes helpful for the instructor to position himself or herself on the ground alongside the horse to help the rider correctly position the horse and apply the aids.This also helps the rider to achieve the correct feel for the movement.
- If working several riders at the same time, it is sometimes helpful to stagger the riding of the movement so that the instructor only has two riders to watch at a time.

FAULTS

- The rider may be confused and ride the movement with the wrong bend or by positioning the horse the wrong way.
- The horse may move easily in the first half of the turn and then evade the last part of the turn by stepping forward out of the movement early.
- The horse may resist and not move away from the leg; sometimes light reinforcement from a schooling whip may help.
- The horse may try to step backwards from the effect of the lateral stepping.
- The horse may become anxious due to a lack of understanding of what is required. Assistance from the ground usually helps in this case.
- The horse may anticipate the turn once he understands the movement.
- He must not be allowed to dictate the movement and move quickly around without accepting the rider's control through the aids.

MORE TURNS ON THE FOREHAND

Arena
20 x 40m or
20 x 60m

Gaits
walk, trot and canter

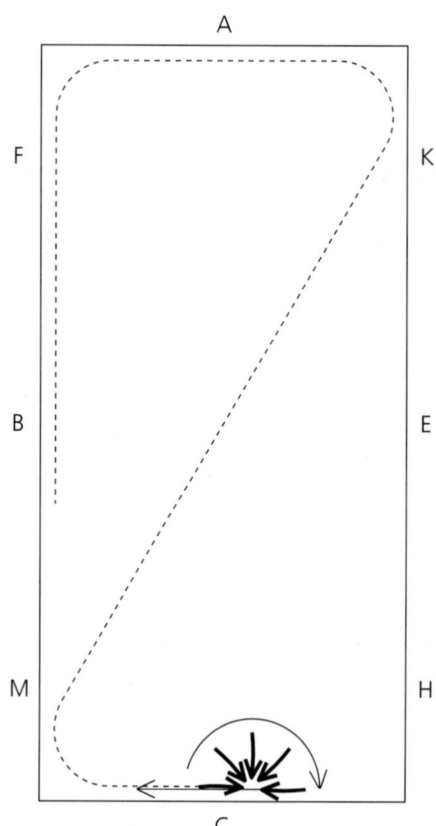

ABOUT THIS EXERCISE

- The exercise can be ridden by individuals or in a group. With a group, it is best ridden in closed order, with leading file going in succession.
- It is most usefully ridden in **trot** but could be ridden in **walk** as the basic pace. **Canter** is involved in the movement.
- The horse is ridden forward actively on one rein in a rhythmical trot. On the first diagonal a change of rein is made.
- At the next marker, either A or C, a halt transition is made.
- From the halt a turn on the forehand through 180° is ridden and the horse is asked to move immediately forward into walk and then make a direct transition to canter. It is acceptable to ride progressively through to canter, if horse or rider lack experience.
- The horse should be ridden away from the turn on the forehand with a forward, rhythmical pace.

AIMS AND BENEFITS

- To improve the responsiveness and obedience of the horse.
- To improve the suppleness and engagement of the horse through the transitions and changes of direction.
- To improve the co-ordination, feel and effect of the rider.
- To provide an interesting and testing series of movements which tie together easily, but will encourage horse and rider to think ahead and

prepare while still focusing on the quality of each component of the whole exercise.

PREPARATION

- The horse must be attentive and moving forward with obedience to the aids.
- The horse must be able to move straight and maintain rhythm in trot and canter.

AIDS AND EXECUTION

- The horse is ridden forward in a rhythmical, active trot.
- The rider makes a well-prepared change of rein across the diagonal line.
- The halt transition is made at A or C.
- The inside rein creates a hint of direction in the gullet (the horse is almost straight).
- The inside leg a little behind the girth asks the hind legs to move over.
- The outside leg controls the hindquarters and regulates the sideways steps; it assists in preventing the horse from stepping backwards.
- The outside rein prevents too much bend in the neck and deters the horse from stepping forwards.
- With the horse very slightly flexed, the inside hind leg steps over and in front of the outside hind leg to bring the horse through a 180° turn within his own length.
- If riding a turn on the forehand to the left the inside hand and leg would be the left hand and leg, the outside hand and leg would be the right hand and leg. In a turn on the forehand to the left the horse is bent to the left.
- After the turn on the forehand, the rider should be aware that the horse is forward and straight (with slight flexion to the new direction) and the aids for canter can then be applied.
- A direct transition from walk to canter comes very easily from the turn on the forehand, because usually the horse is very much on the aids and answers the canter aid cleanly and in good balance.
- If ridden individually, the rider could choose the diagonal to commence the exercise. Each component of the work should then follow on.
- If ridden in a group, the leading file in succession would move off in trot and make the change of rein across the first diagonal approached; the halt would then be made at A or C, and the turn on the forehand would follow. The strike-off into canter would be completed before the rest of the ride had caught up; the rider would then have the whole school in which to execute his canter work before taking the rear of the ride.

RELEVANT TEACHING POINTS

- With groups it is important to keep the ride organised in closed order if each rider is to have enough room to carry out this exercise effectively.
- The instructor should be aware of the position of the rest of the ride and if necessary halt them if the individual is not clear of A or C as they approach.

FAULTS

- Most commonly the rider will have too much bend in the horse's neck in the turn on the forehand. This will unbalance the horse and render the correct execution of the movement more difficult. Position of the instructor on the ground can help to correct this.
- The rider may be slow to prepare each section of the exercise. A lack of preparation will have a cumulative effect on the deterioration of the work.
- In a group situation the horse may hurry the canter in his desire to join his friends at the rear of the ride.

WORK TOWARDS WALK PIROUETTES

Arena
20 x 40m or
20 x 60m

Gait
walk

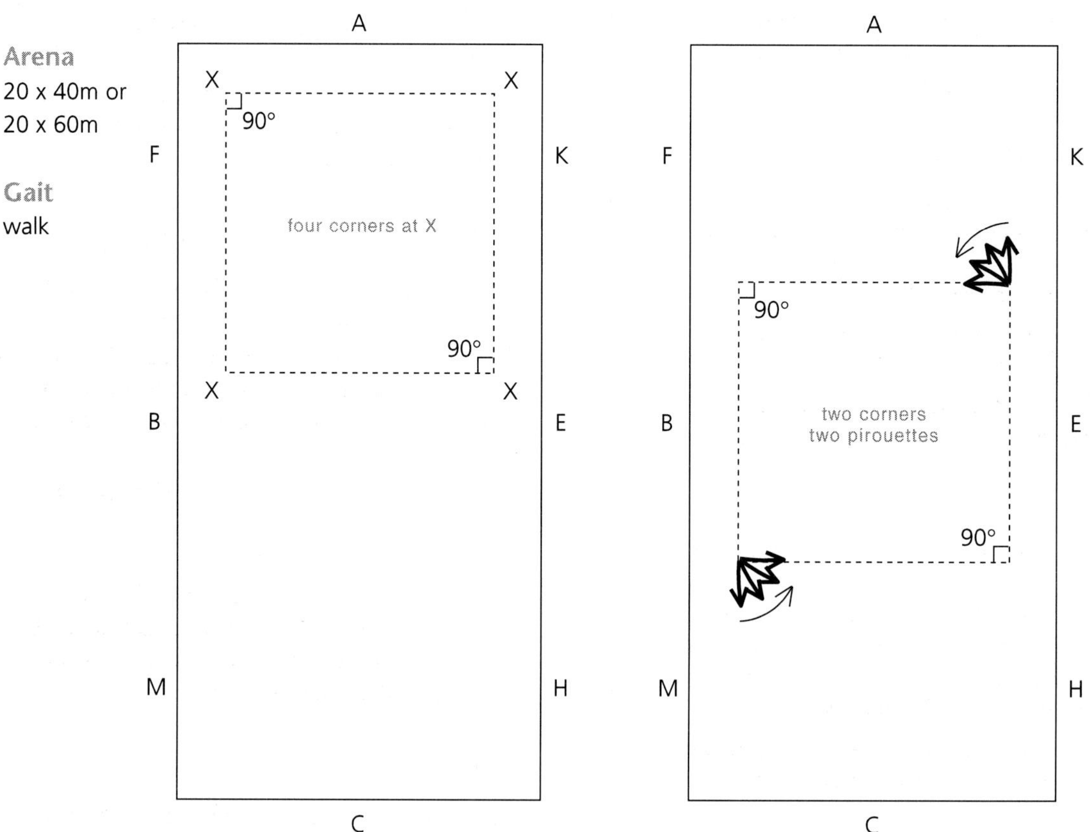

ABOUT THIS EXERCISE

- The exercise is ridden on a square in **walk**; the square can be positioned anywhere in the school (see diagrams), which can be 20 x 40m or 20 x 60m.
- At first the square is ridden with good right-angled corners.
- As the exercise develops the corners are ridden as quarter pirouettes (as shown in second diagram).
- First, one pirouette can be ridden, then two and so on, building up to four maximum.
- At any stage the rider can decide to ride a well-ridden square corner to rebalance the horse, or to give a young horse a 'breather' from the exercise, or to ride a quarter pirouette.
- Similarly with a less experienced rider there is no requirement to ride more pirouettes than the rider has time or experience to prepare.
- The exercise can be ridden individually or in a group. If there are several riders then they should work in open order.

AIMS AND BENEFITS

- To teach the horse further obedience to the lateral aids.
- To improve the carrying power of the hindquarters and thus improve collection.
- To improve the lateral suppleness of the horse.

- As the hindquarters lower and take more weight, the shoulders become lighter and are carried with greater freedom.

PREPARATION

- Begin by riding an accurate square in walk with four good corners, as near to right angles as the horse can manage, without losing rhythm and freedom in the walk.
- Make sure that the horse is obedient and actively in front of the rider's leg.
- The rider should maintain a good position so that the aids will be clearly applied.

AIDS AND EXECUTION

- The corners of the square are ridden with the inside leg on the girth maintaining impulsion, the outside leg controlling the quarters, the inside rein creating the direction and the outside rein controlling the degree of bend, particularly through the head and neck.
- In developing the square corner into a quarter pirouette, half-halts are made as the corner is approached.
- The half-halts prepare the horse, make the walk steps rounder and bring the hind legs more under the horse.
- As the corner is reached the inside rein may be used in a slightly opening way to lead the forehand around.
- At the same time the rider's outside leg should be firmly behind the girth to encourage the hind legs to keep the rhythm of the walk steps almost on the same spot.
- The inside leg keeps a lively activity of the horse's inside hind leg while the outside rein controls the bend in the neck and assists in keeping the movement stepping around on the spot by not allowing the horse to travel forwards too much.
- After two or three pirouette steps through the corner (90°) the forward walk steps are re-established on a straight line away from the corner.
- At the next corner a well-ridden corner can be negotiated or another pirouette depending on ability of horse and rider.

RELEVANT TEACHING POINTS

- The fluency of the walk should be maintained before and after the pirouette steps.
- If tension or anxiety become apparent then the instructor should encourage a return to riding easier corners to restore confidence in horse or rider.
- The rhythm and clarity of the walk is always of great importance and must be carefully monitored and maintained.
- It is important to vary collecting work in walk with plenty of more forward work in trot and/or canter, so that the quality of the walk is never compromised nor impulsion lost.

FAULTS

- The rhythm or quality of the walk may be at risk if the horse is not active enough in the hind legs to begin this work correctly.
- The rider may over-shorten the horse through too much rein and not enough leg, whereby the quality of the walk may be affected.
- Within the pirouette the hind legs may try to escape by swinging outwards, in which case the rider must use more outside leg.
- The horse may walk forward too much through the movement, so avoiding taking more weight on the hind legs and not really producing engaged pirouette steps. In this case more care may be needed with the half-halts to prepare the horse and more regulation with the outside rein.
- Too much bend in the neck through the quarter pirouette will cause a loss of balance and the horse will not be able to take enough weight into the hind legs to free the shoulder.

SIMPLE LEG YIELDING

Arena
20 x 40m or
20 x 60m

Gaits
walk and trot

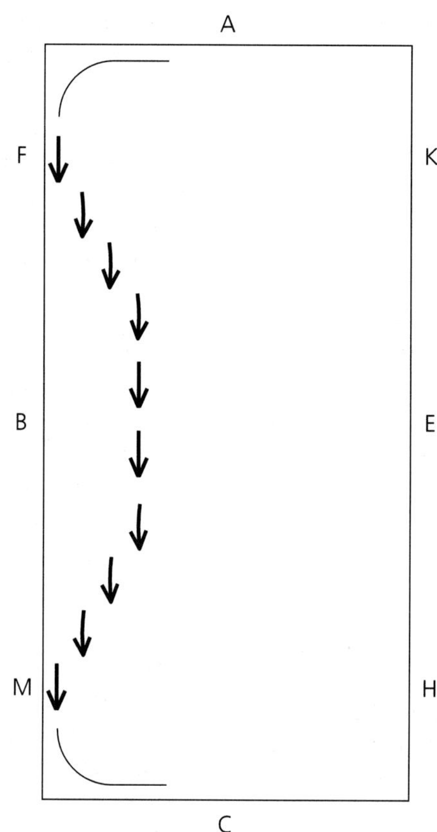

ABOUT THIS EXERCISE

- Leg yielding is a lateral movement where the horse is asked to move forwards and sideways at the same time. It does not require the horse to be collected as it is carried out with the horse almost straight, with just a hint of flexion in the neck away from the direction of movement.
- The horse is asked to move away from the rider's inside leg for a few steps, forwards and sideways away from the direction of the flexion.
- The horse is then asked to move forwards only, straight.
- The flexion is then changed and the horse is asked to move back to the original track from the rider's new inside leg.
- The horse's body is straight throughout the movement, with only the slightest suggestion of flexion in the neck away from the direction of movement.
- The exercise can be usefully ridden in **walk** or **trot**.
- The exercise can be ridden by individuals or in groups, with the riders working in open order.

AIMS AND BENEFITS

- The horse is asked to move with some lateral (sideways) as well as forwards movement.
- The lateral movement helps to increase obedience to the aids.
- Develops the horse's scope and understanding.
- The movement helps to improve suppleness, flexibility and engagement.

- The exercise improves the understanding and co-ordination of the rider.
- The movement is a good stepping stone for horse and rider towards more demanding lateral movements.

PREPARATION

- The horse must be forward and on the aids.
- In **walk** there is more time for horse and/or rider to think out the work and the aids and therefore prevent evasions.
- In **trot** the natural forwardness of the faster pace sometimes helps the movement to be ridden more freely and easily.
- The horse must be as straight as possible.
- A good corner must be ridden to prepare the horse for the aids for leg yield.

AIDS AND EXECUTION

- The inside leg or inside rein always refers to the leg or hand relating to the way the horse is bent. If the horse is bent, say, to the left, the inside leg and inside rein are the left leg and hand.
- If riding the exercise as illustrated, on the left rein, the first corner would be ridden accurately.
- At the first quarter marker, the rider asks for a hint of flexion to the right.
- The rider keeps the horse forward and straight by using the left leg (outside leg) a little behind the girth, while the left rein (outside rein) controls the degree of flexion and the speed of the pace.
- The right leg (inside leg) is applied either on the girth or a fraction behind it, to encourage the horse to move away from it.
- The right rein (inside rein) asks for a little flexion in the neck (through the gullet) so that it is possible to see the horse's right eyelash and no more.
- The horse is asked to move forwards and sideways away from the track, with his body staying parallel to the track.
- After a few steps, the horse is asked to move straight forward again for a few more steps to confirm the straightness.
- The flexion is then changed to the left and the horse is asked to leg yield back to the track.
- The inside leg and hand are now the left hand and leg, and the outside hand and leg are now the right hand and leg.

RELEVANT TEACHING POINTS

- It is very important to stand in such a position that the straightness of the horse (and rider) can be observed. Usually, standing in front of the horse affords the best view.
- The accuracy of the corner is important.
- Positioning the horse straight before asking him to move sideways, is vital.
- The sideways movement must always be in **addition** to the forward movement, **never** instead of it.
- If ridden as a group exercise, sufficient space must be left between each rider that horses do not 'follow' the one in front, and that there is time and space to give individual help and advice to each rider.

FAULTS

- The commonest fault is that the horse is allowed to lose straightness, usually by falling out through the outside shoulder. The value of the exercise is then partly or completely lost.
- Falling out through the shoulder is easily corrected by better control with the outside rein, which can prevent the horse from bending excessively through the neck.
- The horse may move sideways more than forwards, so losing some of the forward movement.
- The horse may quicken in the speed of the rhythm of the pace, particularly in trot.
- The horse may anticipate the movement and move away before the rider has applied the aids.

CENTRE LINE LEG YIELDING

Arena
20 x 40m or
20 x 60m

Gaits
walk or trot

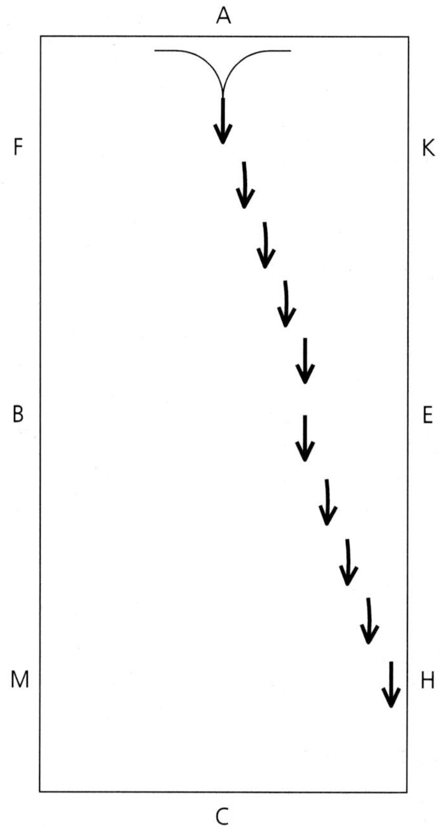

ABOUT THIS EXERCISE

- The exercise is a variation on the last, but in this case the movement is ridden from the centre line, which makes it a little more difficult.
- A turn is made onto the centre line from either rein.
- The horse is ridden straight.
- The flexion is chosen and the leg yield is ridden (away from the direction of the flexion).
- The horse is straightened and ridden forwards.
- Flexion is confirmed and the horse is asked again to move sideways in the same direction as before.
- Straightness is reaffirmed and the horse is ridden forward on the outside track.
- The exercise can be ridden usefully in **walk** and **trot**.
- It can be used for individuals or groups of riders, working in open order.

AIMS AND BENEFITS

- All the reasons for using the previous exercise apply again here.
- It encourages quick obedience and fluency from the horse.
- It is an exercise which helps the rider to feel the straightness of the horse and to control the forwards and sideways steps.

PREPARATION

- The rider must ride a careful turn onto the centre line.
- Care must be taken to keep the horse straight on the centre line before asking for the sideways movement.
- The pace must be active and rhythmical.
- The horse must be obedient and listening to the rider, ready to obey the aids.

AIDS AND EXECUTION

- The aids are applied as for the previous exercise, choosing whether to move from the left leg or right leg in leg yield, the horse is put into the appropriate flexion away from the direction of movement.
- If in left flexion the leg yield will be from the rider's left inside leg.
- The horse is then straightened, ridden forward for a few steps and then asked to move into leg yield again.
- At the end of the movement, the horse is ridden straight and into a clear turn at the end of the school onto either left or right rein.
- The movement is most easily ridden, for example, thus: onto the centre line from the left rein, leg yield from the left leg, straighten, leg yield from the left leg again, straighten and turn left onto the track.
- The movement is made slightly more difficult by turning, for example, onto the centre line from the left rein, leg yielding from the right leg, straighten, leg yield again from the right leg and then straighten and turn left onto the outside track.
- In both these examples, a 20 x 60m school makes the movement easier, as the centre line is longer, giving more room for manoeuvre.

RELEVANT TEACHING POINTS

- It is easier for the horse to have too much bend in the neck when the leg yield is made without changing the flexion – for example, left turn onto the centre, then leg yield from the left leg.
- In changing the flexion, it is more likely that the rider will straighten the horse.
- The teacher must stand in a position where he/she can observe the straightness of both horse and rider.
- The rider must be encouraged to work evenly on both reins, approaching the centre line from both directions.

FAULTS

- The commonest fault is a tendency for the horse to fall out through the outside shoulder. The rider must therefore be encouraged to recognise when the shoulder falls out and use more outside rein to correct this.
- The horse starts to anticipate and not wait for the aids. The exercise must not be repeated too frequently without variation in the work.

MORE CENTRE LINE LEG YIELDING

Arena
20 x 60m

Gaits
walk or trot

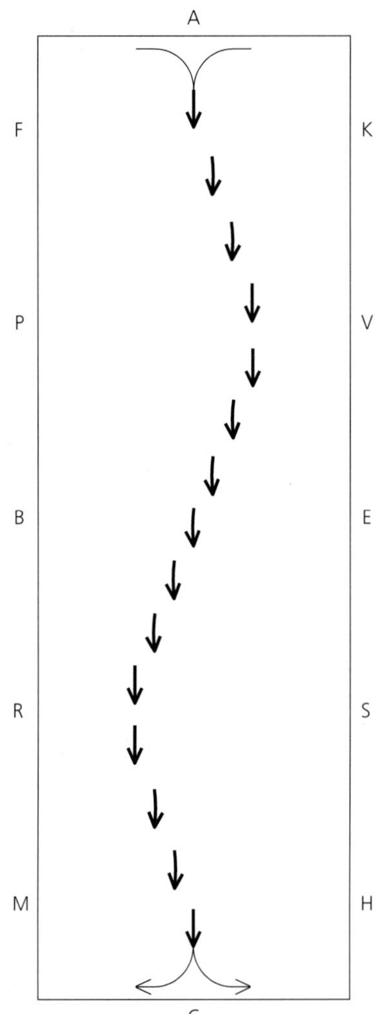

ABOUT THIS EXERCISE

- The exercise can be ridden usefully in **walk** or **trot**.
- The exercise can be ridden by individuals or by groups of riders working in open order.
- A turn is made onto the centre line from either left or right.
- The horse is ridden straight for a few strides.
- Flexion is established, say, to the left, and the horse is moved in leg yield away from the left leg, for a few steps.
- The horse is straightened and ridden forward only.
- The flexion is changed and the horse is moved in leg yield the other way (in this instance to the right) for a few steps.
- The horse is straightened and ridden forward only.
- The flexion is changed again and the horse is asked to move away from the original leg again (i.e. the left leg).
- The horse is straightened and ridden forward before making a turn onto the outside track to go large.

AIMS AND BENEFITS

- The exercise carries all the benefits of the previous two movements, and further develops obedience and good reaction to the rider's aids.
- The exercise further enhances the co-ordination and timing of the rider's aids.
- The exercise helps to prevent the horse from anticipating and reacting in advance of the rider's aids.
- The exercise can help develop the rider's awareness of straightness and feel for the leg yielding movement.

PREPARATION

- The pace (either **walk** or **trot**) should be forward and rhythmical.
- The horse must be on the aids or in front of the rider's legs.
- Care must be taken to ride an accurate turn onto the centre line.
- Turns should be practised from both directions equally.
- The horse must be straight and forward on the centre line before commencing the sideways movement.
- The rider should look up and think ahead to be able to prepare the horse adequately.

AIDS AND EXECUTION

- Turn onto the centre line and maintain a straight, forward-going pace.
- Creating the slightest flexion (in the neck or gullet) with the inside rein, ask the horse to move sideways from the inside leg. Note: if flexion is to the right, the inside leg and hand are the right hand and leg, and vice versa.
- As moving the horse sideways, forward movement **must** be maintained as before. The sideways movement is then in addition to the forward movement, **not** instead of it.
- After a few steps sideways, straighten the horse by reducing the increased sideways pressure of the inside leg and reinforce the outside leg to tell the horse to go forward only.
- After a few strides straight, change the flexion to the opposite direction and repeat the few sideways steps away from the rider's opposite leg.
- This can be repeated three times at least in a 20 x 60m school, but in a 20 x 40m school, it will probably only be possible to establish a few steps of leg yield in each direction.

RELEVANT TEACHING POINTS

- The position of the instructor is all-important in assisting the rider to be aware of the horse's straightness. Just off the centre line, observing the horse(s) coming towards you is ideal.
- Encourage the rider not to hurry the horse through the changes of flexion.
- Emphasis must be on the establishment of the straightness and quiet change of flexion with control of the sideways steps, rather than on extravagant movement away from the rider's leg, which might lack control or accuracy.
- Make sure that riders working in open order give each other enough space, so that the horse is not tempted to be influenced by the horse in front.

FAULTS

- Lack of straightness is a common fault.
- The horse may anticipate the sideways movement and fall out through the outside shoulder, thus reducing the effect of the stepping through of the inside hind leg.
- The horse may move more sideways than forwards – the sideways movement then happens at the expense of the forward movement, which renders the sideways movement of little benefit to the horse.
- The horse anticipates the turn at the end of the centre line and falls around the corner, taking the weight on the inside shoulder, instead of stepping through with the inside hind leg to support the shoulder.

LEG YIELD ON THE DIAGONAL LINE

Arena
20 x 40m or
20 x 60m

Gaits

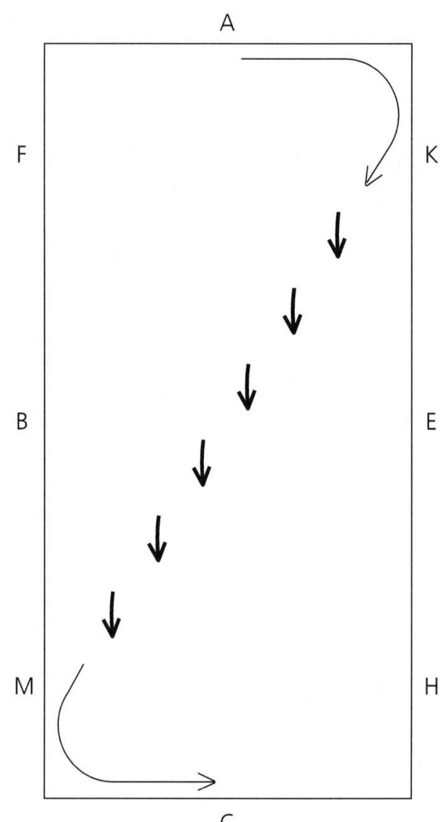

ABOUT THIS EXERCISE

- The exercise can be usefully ridden in **walk** or **trot**.
- It can be ridden individually or in groups, with riders working in open order.
- The horse is turned onto a long diagonal line from either rein.
- The horse must be moving forward in a good rhythm and straight.
- Slight flexion is asked for and leg yielding along the diagonal line.
- The horse's forelegs follow the line of the diagonal and the inside hind leg crosses over and in front of the outside hind leg. The horse's body is almost straight except for a hint of flexion in the gullet away from the direction of the movement.
- The horse is straightened and ridden away from the diagonal onto the outside track.

AIMS AND BENEFITS

- To further develop the obedience and response of the horse to the aids for leg yield.
- To consolidate all the benefits previously described for leg yielding.
- To develop the rider's range of suppling exercises to use for training.
- To add variety for the horse in using leg yield in different ways.

PREPARATION

- The horse must be moving in the chosen gait with forwardness and rhythm.
- The horse must be straight and accepting the flexion away from the direction of movement.
- A good corner should be ridden before turning onto the desired diagonal line.
- The horse's forehand should be directed clearly along the diagonal line.

AIDS AND EXECUTION

- The aids for leg yield are as described in previous exercises.
- The horse is maintained straight but a very slight flexion is asked for with the inside rein.
- The inside leg then asks the horse to move sideways while the forward movement is maintained by the outside leg. The inside leg should be applied very slightly behind the girth but not in such a way that the hindquarters are pushed out.
- Forward movement **must** be maintained – the sideways movement is in addition to the forward movement **never** instead of it.

RELEVANT TEACHING POINTS

- Leg yield on the diagonal is a useful way to assess the true influence of the rider.
- Moving the horse towards the track from a threequarter line or even from the centre line often enables the horse quickly to anticipate the exercise. However, since diagonal lines are used for many purposes, such as basic changes of rein, lengthened strides or medium and extended paces, the horse is less likely to anticipate leg yield.
- The instructor must be in a position to assess the straightness of the horse and the application of the rider's aids. Standing a little to the side of the diagonal line, with the horse approaching, is probably the most useful.
- Most of the points mentioned in previous leg yield exercises also apply here.

FAULTS

- Most of the faults already described for leg yield apply here.
- The rider fails to maintain the diagonal line accurately.
- The horse falls out through the shoulder so evading effective use of the inside hind leg.
- The rider loses straightness in his position, sitting to the outside of the saddle or collapsing the inside hip. If the rider is not straight, it is more difficult for the horse to carry the rider's weight and to move in a balanced way.
- The horse moves too much sideways at the expense of the forward movement.

DIAGONAL LEG YIELD WITH A TRANSITION

Arena
20 x 40m or
20 x 60m

Gaits
trot

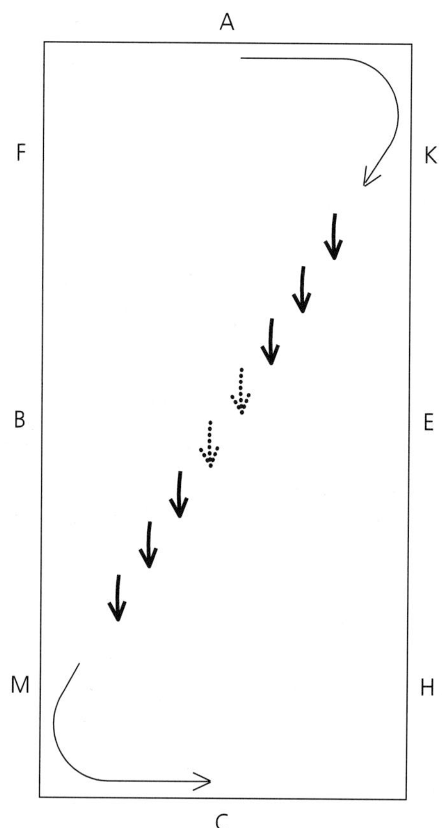

ABOUT THIS EXERCISE

- This exercise is ridden exactly as the one before except that a transition is included within the leg yield, over X.
- The exercise is most usefully ridden in **trot**.
- The exercise can be ridden individually or in groups.
- If working with groups, riders must be in open order, with sufficient space between riders to allow a transition to be ridden down and up again without affecting another rider.

AIMS AND BENEFITS

- All the aims for previous leg yield exercises apply.
- To promote obedience from the horse through the use of the transition within the movement.
- To impress upon the rider the need for well-prepared clear aids.
- Via the transition to obtain further engagement from the horse – as the hind legs step more under the horse in the transition weight is brought off the forehand.

PREPARATION

- All the points of preparation for previous leg yield exercises apply.
- The horse must be forward and fluent in the leg yield.
- The rider must think ahead well to ride a fluent transition.

- The horse must be on the aids.

AIDS AND EXECUTION

- All the aids previously described for leg yield apply here.
- The horse is moving fluently across the diagonal in leg yield.
- The rider makes a preparatory half-halt to warn the horse of the impending transition aid.
- The rider maintains both legs in the position for applying aids for leg yield.
- A closing hand on both reins effects the downward transition to walk.
- As the rider feels the first walk step, he should continue to move the horse forwards and sideways in the leg yield steps into an established rhythm.
- After a few steps of leg yield in walk, the rider asks the horse to move forward into trot, still within the leg yield position, and proceeds along the diagonal in a rhythmical trot.

RELEVANT TEACHING POINTS

- All the points mentioned in the previous exercise apply here.
- The instructor must encourage groups of riders to maintain good spacing so that the transition can be ridden without impeding other riders.
- The instructor needs to encourage riders to be aware of good timing for the transition.
- The horse must be attentive and receptive to the aids for the transition so that there is no loss of harmony through the changes of pace.

FAULTS

- The horse may lose rhythm through the change of pace.
- The horse may try to avoid continuing in sideways steps while making the transition – this is to avoid stepping through actively with the inside hind leg.
- The horse may hollow and come above the bit during the transition where he has to work harder to maintain roundness.
- The horse may slow down either before the transition or after the return to trot – in both cases this is to avoid having to maintain active hind legs through the changes of pace.

LEG YIELD WITH HALF CIRCLES

Arena
20 x 40m or
20 x 60m

Gaits
walk or trot

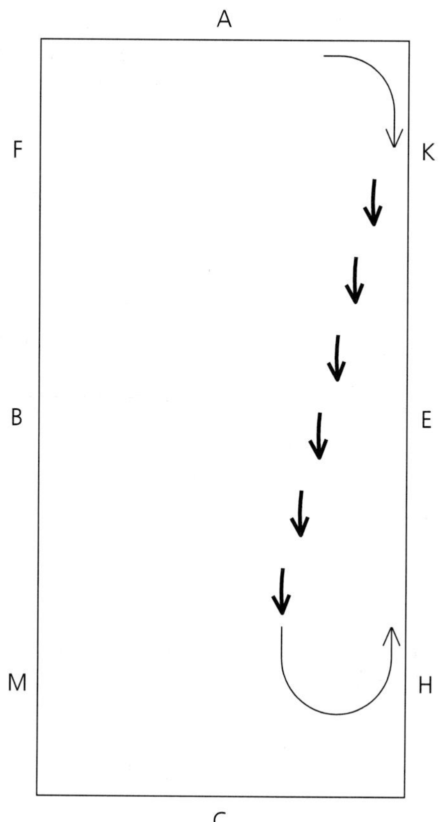

ABOUT THIS EXERCISE

- The exercise can be usefully ridden in **walk** or **trot**.
- The exercise can be ridden by individuals or groups of riders in open order.
- From the first quarter marker on the long side the flexion is changed and the horse is asked to move in leg yield away from the outside track.
- After a few steps the horse is straightened and immediately ridden into a small half circle to return to the track.
- The exercise involves a change of rein each time it is ridden.
- The exercise can and should be ridden equally on both reins.

AIMS AND BENEFITS

- The main aims of leg yielding work have already been listed under the preceding exercises.
- To enable a change of rein to be made via a different method.
- To improve lateral suppleness and engagement in the horse.
- To help the rider develop feel and effect.

PREPARATION

- The horse must be moving forward in a good rhythm in the chosen gait.
- In **walk** the rider has more time to think ahead and prepare.
- In **trot** there is more natural forward movement

and because of that the exercise may be more fluently ridden.

- The corner must be ridden with care and accuracy.
- The horse must be obedient to the aids.

AIDS AND EXECUTION

- The usual aids for leg yield apply (as described in earlier leg yield exercises).
- On deciding how many leg yield steps will be ridden, the rider then consciously straightens the horse by increasing the pressure of the outside leg and slightly reducing the sideways pressure of the inside leg.
- The inside flexion can be maintained as it is then directed into the half circle.
- The half circle is effected by the inside leg maintaining support on the girth to provide forward movement, and the outside leg guarding the hindquarters a little behind the girth to stop them escaping.
- The inside rein creates the direction and bend for the half circle.
- The outside rein controls the degree of bend through the neck and also regulates the forward movement.

RELEVANT TEACHING POINTS

- Positioning of the instructor is all-important, particularly if teaching a group of riders. A little off the track on the long side where the leg yield is being ridden, would be most helpful. In this position you can advise on the straightness of the horse in the leg yield and then the control of the bend through the half circle.
- Make riders aware of the need to maintain sufficient distance so that each is able to ride the half circle without interference from another.
- Make the ride aware that horses will be working in opposite directions on some occasions, so riders should stay alert and be ready to pass another rider left hand to left hand.
- The rider's inside leg should never slip so far back that there is a risk of the horse swinging his quarters out, away from the leg and therefore losing straightness.
- The position of the rider's inside leg as described applies to all the leg yield exercises covered to this point.

FAULTS

- The faults discussed in all previous leg yield exercises apply here.
- The horse may fall out through the shoulder or the quarters on the half circle.
- The half circle may be very small if the horse has not leg yielded very freely away from the track.

LEG YIELD AND TURN ON THE FOREHAND

Arena
20 x 40m or
20 x 60m

Gaits
walk or trot

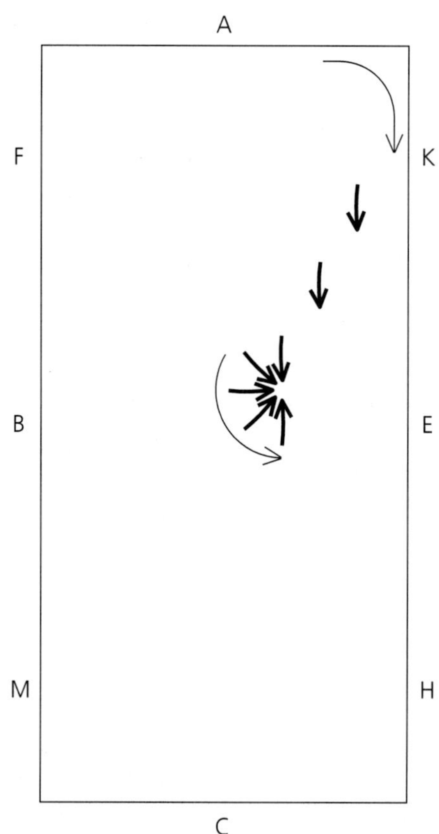

ABOUT THIS EXERCISE

- This exercise begins exactly like the previous one.
- The exercise can be ridden in **walk** or **trot**.
- It can be ridden individually or in groups of riders in open order.
- The leg yield commences from the first quarter marker after the corner.
- The horse is asked to leg yield away from the wall/track towards the centre of the school.
- After a few steps the horse may be halted and a turn on the forehand ridden, or a turn about the forehand can be ridden from walk.
- Once the horse has made a 180° turn, he is ridden forward and straight on the inner track.
- The horse may be asked for leg yield to return to the outside track.
- The horse may be ridden straight to the end of the school where a turn is made back onto the outside track.
- The horse may be ridden from the turn on the forehand (or turn about the forehand) onto a straight diagonal line to return to the outside track.

AIMS AND BENEFITS

- All the points of benefit mentioned in the previous leg yield exercises apply to this exercise.
- Through the turn on the forehand, to add

another dimension of obedience to the aids.

- To encourage greater feel and co-ordination from the rider.
- To provide variety and interest for both horse and rider.
- To increase suppleness.

PREPARATION

- The preparation for this exercise is as described in the previous one.
- The **walk** or **trot** should be forward going and rhythmical.
- A good corner is essential – the horse must be on the aids and obedient to the change in flexion after the good corner.
- Straightness is essential.
- A few steps of leg yield are ridden and then a halt transition if turn on the forehand is to be ridden.
- When riding a turn about the forehand the movement will be ridden from walk.

AIDS AND EXECUTION

- The aids for leg yield are as previously described.
- The horse is moved away from the track in a few steps of leg yield.
- If in trot, a transition to walk is made.
- To make a turn about the forehand a half-halt is ridden to prepare the horse.
- The inside rein maintains a hint of flexion in the neck (only enough to see the horse's eyelash.)
- The inside leg applies pressure a little behind the girth to move the quarters around.
- The outside rein controls the degree of bend in the neck and prevents the horse from stepping forwards.
- The outside leg behind the girth controls the speed with which the horse steps sideways and prevents the quarters from swinging out.
- The horse is moved forward and straight after completing a 180° turn.
- A decision is made as to the method by which the horse is ridden back to the track if required.
- In a turn about the forehand, the horse should negotiate the turn without coming completely to halt.
- In turn on the forehand the horse halts and the movement involves the horse pivoting on the inside foreleg through the turn.

RELEVANT TEACHING POINTS

- All the points relevant to leg yield apply to the first part of this exercise.
- In the turn on the forehand or turn about the forehand, it may be necessary for the instructor to position himself close to the horse, to assist the rider with a steadying hand on the bridle to prevent too much bend in the neck or stop the horse from moving forward.
- In this position it is also possible to help reinforce the rider's inside leg to help him move the horse sideways,
- In group sessions it is sensible to limit the riding of the turns to two or three riders at a time, so that the instructor can watch and assist each rider more effectively.

FAULTS

- The faults likely to occur in leg yield have been well listed in previous exercises.
- The most common faults in turn on or about the forehand are the horse bending too much in the neck and so losing balance and not stepping through with the inside hind leg.
- The horse may swing his hindquarters around too quickly and not be fully under the control of the rider.
- The horse may negotiate half or two thirds of the turn and then walk out of the last part of the turn so evading the influence of the inside hind leg.

LEG YIELD WITH CANTER

Arena
20 x 40m or
20 x 60m

Gaits
walk, trot and canter

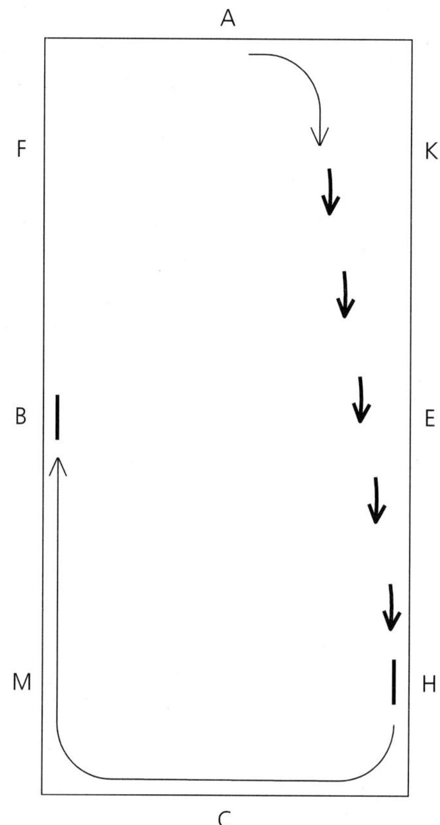

ABOUT THIS EXERCISE

- This exercise is most usefully ridden in **trot** and **canter** but could be performed in **walk** and **trot**.
- The exercise can be ridden individually but is particularly appropriate for groups of riders working in open order on the same rein.
- In the chosen gait, the rider makes a turn onto the threequarter line and from here leg yields back to the outside track.
- On reaching the track at approximately the second quarter marker, a transition to canter is made.
- Canter is maintained around the short side and to the next half marker.
- Transition to trot is made and the horse is then re-balanced as necessary to repeat the exercise.

AIMS AND BENEFITS

- The exercise combines the already listed benefits of leg yield with transitions to and from canter.
- To improve the obedience of the horse.
- To focus the rider's mind on a series of accurate aids based on good preparation and thinking ahead.
- To improve the rider's feel and awareness of rhythm, balance, straightness and impulsion.
- To improve the rider's ability to be aware of other riders and maintain good working distances from other horses.

- Through the leg yield, to engage the horse's inside hind leg, which in turn helps puts him in a better balance to respond to the canter aid.
- To improve the quality of the canter and downward transition – with only one short side in canter before asking for a transition back to trot, the canter is often in a better balance, and in the downward transition the horse is less inclined to run onto the forehand.

PREPARATION

Describing the exercise as most usefully ridden in trot:

- The trot must be forward going, rhythmical and the horse on the aids.
- A good corner is ridden onto the threequarter line and straightness is assured first.
- Care must be taken to ride each part of the exercise with good preparation by thinking ahead.

AIDS AND EXECUTION

- The aids for each part of this exercise have been previously described in other movements.

RELEVANT TEACHING POINTS

- It is important that the rider is aware that if any phase of the exercise begins to deteriorate then he is not committed to ride into the next part. For example, if the leg yield is poor, the rider does not need to ask for canter.
- The exercise is such that at any point within it the rider can decide to repair faults which may be occurring, rather than commit himself to the next phase of the movement.
- The instructor should stand in such a position that he/she can observe the straightness of the line and the leg yield.

FAULTS

- The horse may fall out through the shoulder on the initial turn onto the threequarter line.
- The horse may anticipate the leg yield and again fall out through the shoulder.
- The horse may ignore the canter aid and run into the transition rather than keeping the weight on his hind legs and therefore engaging through the transition.
- The horse may hurry away from the canter-to-trot transition, and it may be helpful to circle and re-balance before re-presenting the horse for the exercise again.
- Riders may tend to get too close to one another and must learn to think ahead and circle away in good time.

TRANSITIONS USING CANTER

Arena
20 x 40m or
20 x 60m

Gaits
trot and canter

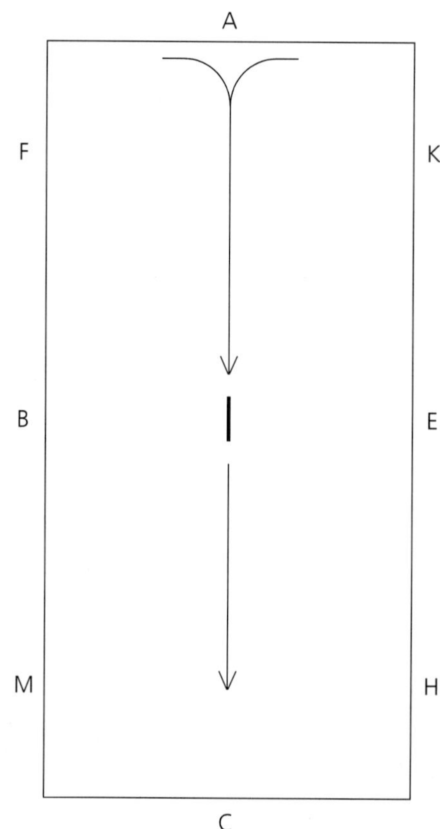

ABOUT THIS EXERCISE

- The exercise is most usefully ridden from **trot**.
- The exercise can be ridden individually or in groups with riders in open order.
- A turn is made onto the centre line from either rein in trot.
- On the centre line a transition is made to right or left canter. The line is continued straight to the bottom of the school, before making a turn to the outside track in the direction of the canter lead established.
- Trot can be re-established somewhere on the next long side and the exercise can be repeated.

AIMS AND BENEFITS

- To help establish more obedient transitions to canter on a straight line.
- To emphasise the rider's need to make the horse straight on the centre line and prepare well for the specific lead required.
- To bring home that the need for straightness on the centre line (or any other line) is essential and that achieving straightness is good preparation for test riding and competing.
- To develop the rider's feel for straightness and timing for applying the aids.

PREPARATION

- The trot must be forward and rhythmical.
- A well-prepared turn is made onto the centre line, maintaining control of the outside shoulder.
- The horse must be ridden forward on the centre line while encouraging him to accept the half-halt and preparation for the desired canter lead.
- Once in canter the horse must be ridden forward again to help maintain straightness.

AIDS AND EXECUTION

- The aids for the canter transition are:

  – inside leg on the girth, for impulsion;

  – inside rein maintaining slight flexion in the direction of movement;

  – outside leg a little behind the girth, controlling the hindquarters and, with a greener horse, giving a clear aid for the strike-off;

  – outside rein controlling the pace and regulating the bend.
- Once in canter the horse needs to be held in a slight 'shoulder fore' position to maintain straightness on the centre.
- A good turn is made back onto the outside track and the rider must plan when to make the downward transition.

RELEVANT TEACHING POINTS

- The instructor needs to stay in a position to watch carefully the turn onto the centre line.
- The quality of the turn and the straightness before the transition will dictate the accuracy and quality of the transition.
- The rider must be made aware of the straightness before and after the transition.
- The rider must be encouraged to decide when to make the downward transition and plan ahead so it can be well prepared.

FAULTS

- The rider may over-shoot the centre line, which will cause problems in straightness.
- The horse may cut the corner onto the centre line, causing the same problems.
- The horse may 'wobble' on the centre line.
- The horse may evade the transition aid by swinging the quarters away, coming above the bit and ignoring the aid, or quickening in the trot.
- The horse may lose straightness immediately after the transition.
- The horse may fall in or out around the corner back onto the track.
- The horse may fall onto the forehand in the downward transition back to trot.

INTRODUCING COUNTER CANTER

Arena
20 x 40m or
20 x 60m

Gait
canter

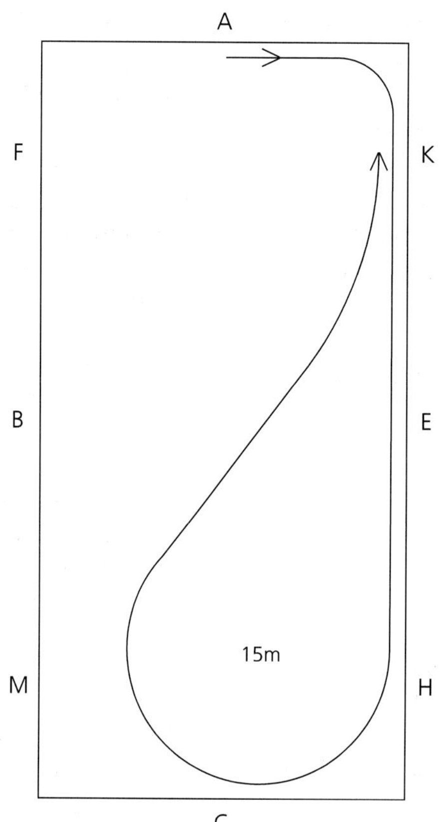

ABOUT THIS EXERCISE

- This exercise is ridden in **canter**.
- The exercise is most easily ridden individually, but can be carried out by small groups of riders (up to four) in open order.
- In canter, a half circle of 15m diameter is ridden from the quarter marker at the end of a long side.
- Canter is ridden back to the track to the first quarter marker on the same long side, the bend is maintained to the leading leg throughout the movement, so the last part of the exercise (see diagram) is in counter canter.
- Trot is re-established at the track.

AIMS AND BENEFITS

- Developing counter canter from a simple change of rein such as this is an easy introduction to the use of counter canter as a suppling and straightening exercise.
- To improve obedience and balance of the horse.
- To improve the co-ordination and timing of the rider's aids.
- To help develop the rider's feel for straightness – straightness in canter is essential.

PREPARATION

- The first simple loop exercises described on page 10 can be ridden in canter to begin introducing the concept of counter canter to horse and rider.

- The **canter** should be rhythmical and forward going.
- The horse should be obedient to the aids for both canter leads.
- It should be easy to make a transition to canter on a straight line as well as in a corner.
- It is helpful if the horse will shorten and lengthen a little in the canter. (See the exercise on page 28.)
- Practise riding 15m circles to assure balance and maintenance of pace.

AIDS AND EXECUTION

- In a well-balanced canter begin the half circle from the second quarter marker.
- Look for the line to be ridden back to the track to the first quarter marker.
- Throughout the riding of the line returning to the track, make sure that the aids are sustained to the leading leg.
- The inside leg on the girth maintains impulsion; the outside leg behind the girth controls the quarters; the inside hand maintains flexion to the leading leg; and the outside hand controls this flexion and regulates the speed of the pace.
- The rider's weight should be very slightly into the inside seat bone.
- As the rider prepares for the downward transition to trot, the transition is made with the outside rein (to the bend of the horse). This will help to establish the correct bend coming into the new direction.

RELEVANT TEACHING POINTS

- Balance and engagement are essential in developing counter canter.
- The horse will not be able to hold his balance in counter canter unless he is sufficiently engaged to sustain easily at least a 15m circle in canter.
- As the rider begins to ride counter canter it is essential that he is aware of the need to maintain his own balance and position over the leading leg of the horse.
- If the rider begins to move his position to follow the direction in which the movement is going, he will unbalance the horse and cause him either to break back to trot, to go disunited in the canter or simply become tense and anxious.
- It is important to emphasise the importance of asking for the downward transition with the outside hand (to the bend of the horse).
- It is important to emphasise the need to engage the horse, and to make a good half-halt in preparation for the downward transition so that the horse comes forward into trot without falling onto his forehand.

FAULTS

- The horse may lose a little balance and become tense in the introduction of a new exercise.
- In counter canter it is critical that the rider does not disturb the balance of the horse as he learns counter canter or the pace itself may be adversely affected.
- The rider must therefore be very aware of his position staying over the leading leg and not shifting his weight as the direction changes.
- The horse may try to quicken as he feels the influence of the counter canter.
- The horse may conversely try to slow down avoiding the engagement.
- If the horse loses balance he may change legs or go disunited in the canter. In both cases he should be brought into a balanced trot and the exercise should be restarted from a good basis, rather than trying to hurry him back into canter regardless of quality.

MORE COUNTER CANTER

Arena
20 x 40m or
20 x 60m

Gait
canter

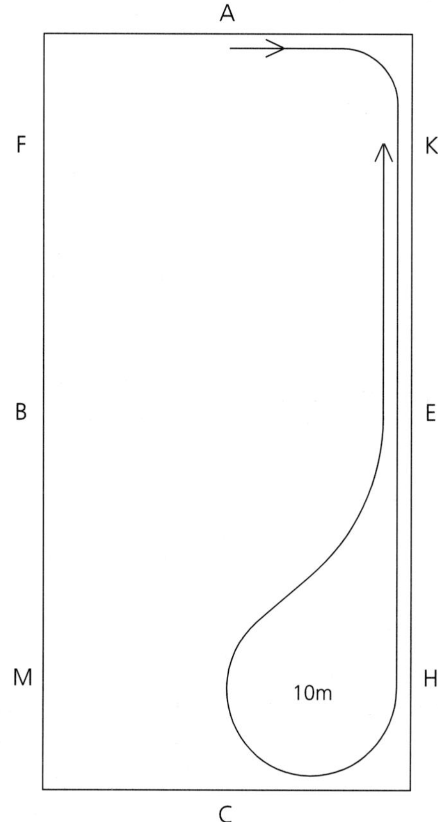

ABOUT THIS EXERCISE

- This exercise can be a development from the previous exercise.
- It can be ridden in **canter** by small groups or individuals.
- The horse makes a half circle of 10m onto the centre line, returning to the track at the half marker.
- The exercise is versatile in that the counter canter is then held for as long as desired or appropriate to the level of horse or rider.

AIMS AND BENEFITS

- All the points of benefit referred to in the previous exercise apply here.
- To progress the ability of the horse and rider in riding counter canter.
- Since the movement is asked for in some dressage tests at higher Novice and lower Elementary level, the exercise helps to familiarise the horse and rider with what might be asked of them in competition.

PREPARATION

- The horse must be confident and secure in maintaining balance, rhythm and impulsion on a 10m circle.
- The horse should be capable of shortening and lengthening the canter while maintaining balance, rhythm and impulsion.

- The horse must be obedient to the aids for canter on both leads on straight lines.
- The horse must be engaged, and the rider should look ahead in preparation for the half 10m circle.
- The rider must maintain a balanced position throughout the movement.

AIDS AND EXECUTION

- The aids are as described for the previous exercise.
- Care must be taken to ride the half circle small enough to negotiate the line back to the half marker.
- The rider should gauge the half circle by looking to the centre line and then back to the half marker.

RELEVANT TEACHING POINTS

- It is important to make sure that there is a greater degree of engagement and balance in the canter before asking for this slightly more difficult movement.
- The rider must be encouraged to ride an accurate 10m half circle as this will make it easier to direct the horse back to the half marker.
- Before he rides the movement, direct the rider as to how long he should endeavour to hold the counter canter; nominate a point in the school.
- Pre-planning the trot transition will help the rider to ride more positively to sustain the counter canter.
- Each time the horse is successful in performing the work, then ask a little more. However, constantly assess the confidence of both horse and rider.
- The rider must ask for the downward transition with the outside hand. This will help bring the horse into the correct bend for the new direction.

FAULTS

- The canter may not be active or balanced enough to sustain the more demanding circle.
- The horse may lose balance and change lead or become disunited.
- The horse may show some tension and this may cause the above faults.
- The rider may change his balance in the return to the track and this may unbalance the horse.
- The rider may be confused about the aids for the downward transition – the outside hand must always relate to the bend of the horse.

INTRODUCING SHOULDER-IN

Arena
20 x 40m or
20 x 60m

Gaits
walk, trot and canter

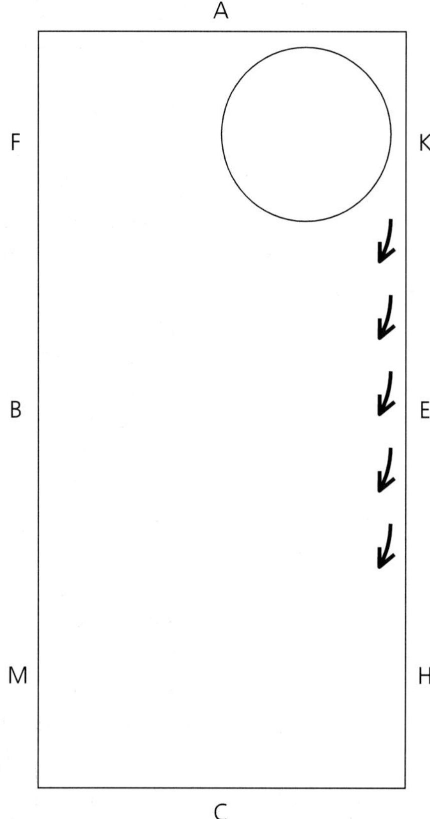

ABOUT THIS EXERCISE

- This exercise is most usefully ridden in **trot** but may be performed in **walk** and **canter**.
- The exercise can be ridden individually or in groups with riders working in open order.
- A 10m circle is ridden at the quarter marker and shoulder-in is established along the long side immediately following the circle.
- Shoulder-in is a lateral exercise where the horse is asked to move forwards and sideways at the same time along a designated line.
- The horse moves away from the direction in which he is bent.
- The exercise demands a degree of collection or engagement to allow the horse to step actively under with his inside hind leg and bend throughout the length of his body.
- The horse's inside foreleg crosses in front of the outside foreleg.
- The inside hind leg steps forward and across under the horse's body and when viewed from in front, the inside hind leg will be in line with the outside foreleg.
- The angle of the shoulder-in will be up to a maximum of 30° from the track. If ridden at a smaller angle, which demands less from the horse, the movement is called shoulder fore and is a useful exercise to help straighten the horse.

AIMS AND BENEFITS

- The exercise is useful to further develop suppleness and engagement of the inside hind leg.

- Shoulder-in is probably the most versatile lateral movement to assist in straightening the horse.
- Shoulder-in can be used to gain submission from an awkward or spooky horse.
- Shoulder-in can be used as a platform from which to develop other lateral movements.
- The exercise helps develop the co-ordination of the rider and correct application of aids.
- The exercise helps develop feel and awareness from the rider.

PREPARATION

- The horse must be going forward with rhythm and activity.
- The horse should be capable of maintaining balance and forward movement on a 10m circle, which should indicate a degree of collection in the gait.
- A good corner must be ridden to maintain the basic criteria described.

AIDS AND EXECUTION

- The circle is ridden accurately with activity and preferably in sitting trot.
- Coming out of the circle the rider should feel as if he is going to ride a second circle; instead he rides a good half-halt.
- The inside leg on the girth motivates the inside hind leg.
- The inside rein asks the shoulders to come off the track and is well supported by the outside rein. Thus the whole of the front of the horse turns, the outside shoulder is contained and the horse does not bend just his head and neck.
- The outside leg holds the quarters and prevents them escaping.
- Once the angle is established the rider directs the horse along the track with a lively inside leg maintaining the position of the shoulder-in, being regulated by the other aids as described.
- The rider should very slightly feel more weight on his inside seat bone.

RELEVANT TEACHING POINTS

- The instructor should be in a position (usually in front of the horse and a little to the inner track) to see the angle of the shoulder-in and notice any evasions from the horse or lack of effect of the rider's aids.
- Advise when a few good steps have been achieved and then encourage the rider to ride straight after the shoulder-in, by using the outside rein and inside leg. (There are other methods of riding away from shoulder-in which will be covered in the next few exercises.)
- As shoulder-in is a method of collecting the horse and increasing engagement, it is important to utilise this greater power in the hind legs with some subsequent, more forward type of exercise.
- Riding into some medium trot steps or into a transition to another pace should reflect the engagement the exercise has achieved.

FAULTS

- The horse bends too much in the neck and leaves his shoulder on the track. If so, more outside rein should be used with slightly less inside rein.
- The horse may slow down and lose impulsion.
- The horse may show some resistance and come above the bit.
- Occasionally there may be too much angle, and then bend through the body is lost.
- The horse may tilt his head to evade the bend. If the outside rein is too strong with insufficient inside leg, this may cause the head to tilt.
- The rider must stay in balance with the movement, with a hint of feeling more weight on his inside seat bone. He should not lean inwards, and his shoulders should follow the horse's shoulders.

SHOULDER-IN AND LENGTHEN

Arena
20 x 40m or
20 x 60m

Gaits
trot

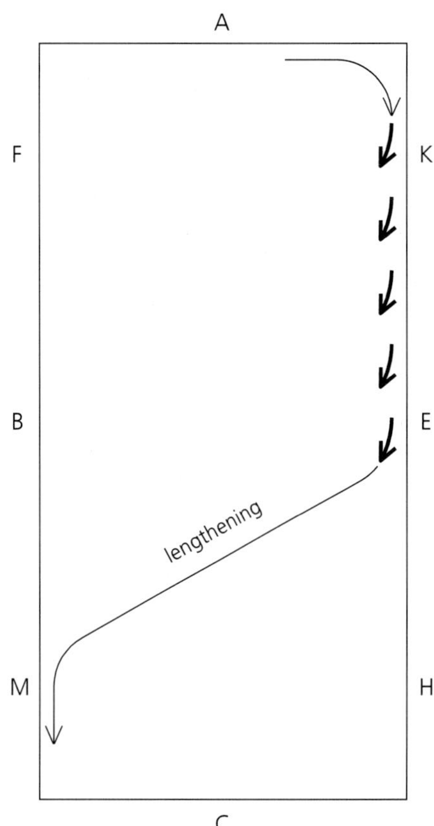

ABOUT THIS EXERCISE

- This exercise is most easily ridden in **trot**.
- The exercise can be used for individuals or for groups of riders in open order.
- Shoulder-in is established along the long side from the quarter marker to the half marker.
- At the half marker the horse is ridden straight onto a diagonal line, towards the opposite quarter marker, across the school.
- Lengthening strides or medium trot is asked for across this line, changing the rein.
- The horse is ridden away onto the opposite rein.
- The exercise can be repeated easily on both reins.
- If the strides are gradually lengthened, then this is known as lengthening the stride; the development of the length is progressive over two or three strides and also in the return.
- If there is a clear transition made into bigger strides and then another clear transition back to working-length strides, then this is known as **medium trot**.
- It is easier for the horse to make the lengthened strides progressively – this is required at Novice dressage level; at Elementary level the requirement would be **medium trot.**

AIMS AND BENEFITS

- The exercise has all the benefits listed for the previous one.
- Shoulder-in engages the hind legs more under

the horse and so efficiently prepares the horse to be able to give some lengthening strides in trot.

- Lengthening the stride from the shoulder-in, is an ideal way to use the concept of shortening, lengthening and shortening again as a means of suppling the horse mentally and physically.
- This exercise is found in some dressage tests of Elementary level. Using it will familiarise the horse with the link between shoulder-in and medium trot.
- The collecting exercise often teaches the horse that he can then open the stride to give bigger steps.

PREPARATION

- The horse must be able to show a small degree of collection, which the exercise should further develop.
- A good corner must be ridden to enable the shoulder-in to be carried out effectively.
- The horse must be going forward calmly and in a good rhythm in trot.

AIDS AND EXECUTION

- The aids for shoulder-in are as described in the last exercise.
- The shoulder-in is ridden from the quarter marker to the half marker on the same side.
- On reaching the half marker, the horse is made straight either on the same long side or made straight onto the diagonal line towards the opposite quarter marker.
- It is slightly easier to straighten and lengthen on the outside track rather than turn onto the diagonal line and lengthen.
- In straightening from shoulder-in, the inside leg is used in conjunction with the outside rein. As the horse is made straight, both legs generate the energy into the lengthening strides.
- A half-halt (or several half-halts) may be necessary to encourage the horse to carry his weight on his hind legs, especially as the lengthening is asked for.
- In this way the bigger steps will feel and appear to be 'uphill', with greater extravagance of the front legs from a more expressive shoulder, as well as more activity from behind.

RELEVANT TEACHING POINTS

- The instructor needs to position himself so he can assist the rider in spotting evasions, such as too much neck bend (in shoulder-in), or hurrying in the lengthening strides. It is preferable to watch the horse coming towards you in this exercise.
- It may be preferable to accept a little less angle in the shoulder-in (shoulder-fore) while keeping, rhythm, balance and harmony.
- Similarly, ask for less extravagant length of stride, but keeping rhythm, balance and harmony. This is a stronger base from which to ask a little more each time.

FAULTS

- The horse may show some resistance in shoulder-in – he may hollow and resist in his frame.
- The horse may give too much bend in the neck and therefore fall out through the outside shoulder.
- If, as described above, the shoulder falls out, then the outside shoulder is against the wall and there is no true shoulder-in position. In this case there is neck bend only and no true engagement of the inside hind leg.
- The horse may slow down in the shoulder-in to evade the energy and engagement.
- The horse may quicken and 'run' off his hind legs onto the forehand in the lengthening strides.
- In the lengthening steps the steps become faster and sometimes shorter and quicker, rather than keeping the same rhythm and becoming bigger and more 'uphill'.
- The horse must stay confident and not become worried by the exercise.

SHOULDER-IN WITH TRANSITION

Arena
20 x 40m or
20 x 60m

Gaits
trot

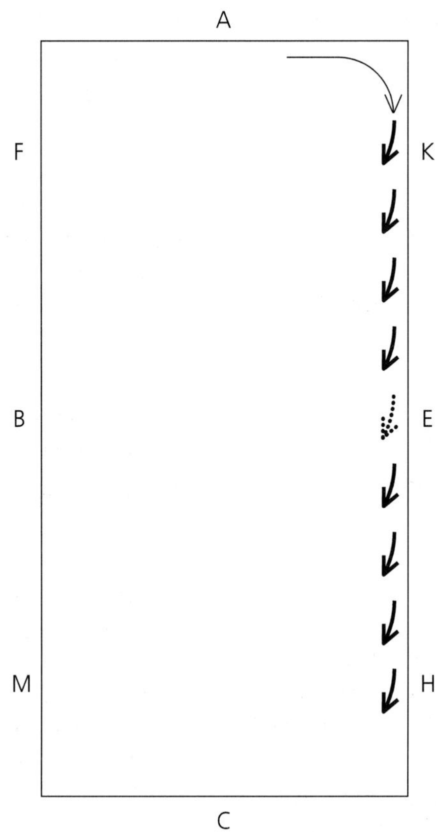

ABOUT THIS EXERCISE

- The exercise is most usefully ridden in **trot** with a transition to **walk** and then a return to **trot**.
- The exercise can be ridden individually and in small groups with the riders in open order.
- The shoulder-in is ridden from the first quarter marker on the long side. Half way along the long side, a transition is made to walk (remaining in shoulder-in) for two or three strides, followed immediately by an upward transition into trot.
- Shoulder-in is continued to the end of the long side.
- The exercise should be ridden on both reins equally.
- The exercise could be ridden on the centre line, where it would be necessary to be more attentive to straightness.

AIMS AND BENEFITS

- The points made in the two previous exercises apply equally here.
- The transition requires obedience from the horse.
- The transition increases the response of the horse to the aids.
- The transition within the shoulder-in movement requires still more engagement of the hindquarters, so improving balance and collection.

- The exercise improves the feel, co-ordination and aid application of the rider.

PREPARATION

- Preparation is as for the previous exercise.
- The horse should be in a good, active, rhythmical trot.
- The horse must be balanced and active through the corner.

AIDS AND EXECUTION

- The aids for shoulder-in are as previously described.
- The horse must be kept active and balanced while the aids for the downward transition are applied.
- The horse should continue to be ridden in a shoulder-in position for two or three strides in walk before the upward transition back into trot is made.
- Co-ordination of the aids in conjunction with feel from the rider are essential in maintaining harmony throughout this movement.

RELEVANT TEACHING POINTS

- All the teaching points mentioned for the past two exercises apply here.
- The instructor should be aware of the need to encourage the rider to make the transition in good time and to be in harmony with the horse.
- The rider may need encouragement to ride purposefully into the transition until the horse understands what is required of him.

FAULTS

- All the faults previously mentioned for shoulder-in may occur in this exercise.
- The horse may show some resistance in the transition, particularly in the down transition.
- The horse may be reluctant to take sideways steps in walk before moving up to trot again.
- The horse may drift forward off the line (or track) because the rider does not make it clear to the horse with the outside rein that he must stay on the line. The control with the outside rein should not be an isolated aid, or other faults may occur.
- All four aids (two legs, two hands) co-ordinate together to produce a fluent, harmonious result.

SHOULDER-IN AWAY FROM THE WALL

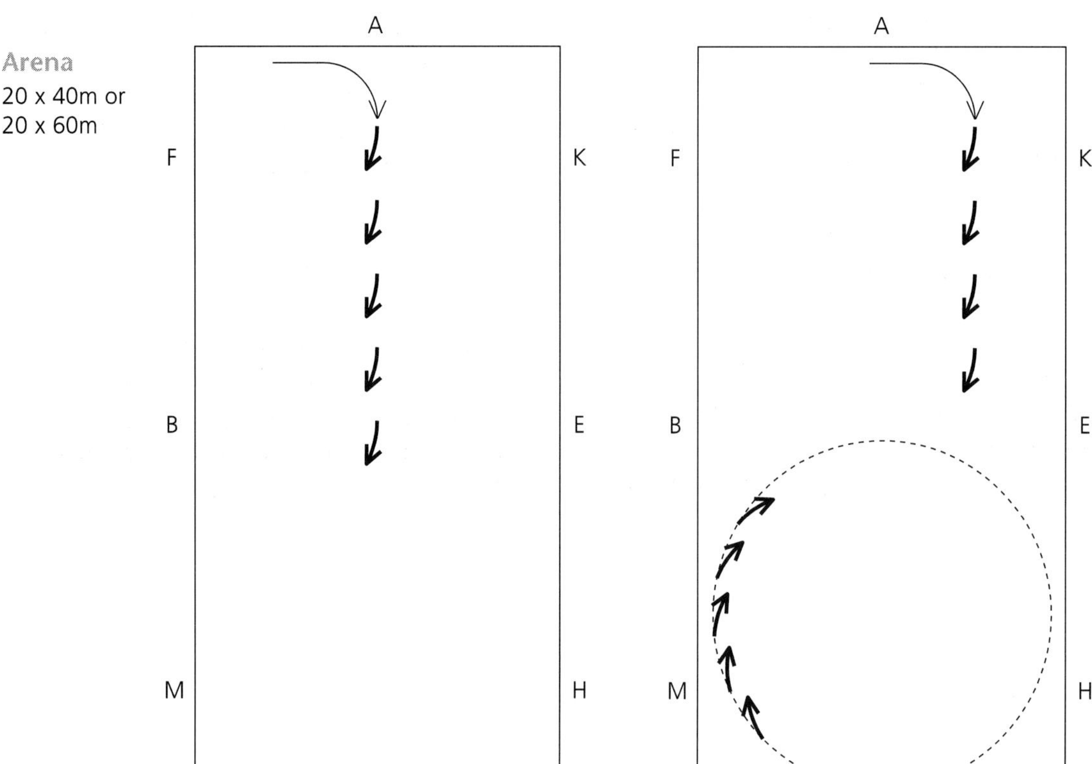

ABOUT THIS EXERCISE

- Shoulder-in is most usefully ridden in **trot**, but can also be ridden to good effect in **walk** and **canter**.
- Shoulder-in can be ridden individually or in groups in open order.
- Shoulder-in can be ridden on the centre line, on the threequarter line or on a circle line.

AIMS AND BENEFITS

- All the points of benefit listed in the last three exercises apply here.
- Shoulder-in or shoulder-fore position can be ridden to good effect as a correcting exercise if the horse is spooking or being reluctant to accept submission due to tension or belligerence.
- Riding shoulder-in on a line not supported by the outside track or wall of the school, encourages the rider to be much more aware of the positioning of the horse.
- Riding shoulder-in off the wall also enables the rider to identify more clearly if the horse is evading and in which direction.

PREPARATION

- All the points of preparation for the previous exercises apply here.
- It is essential for the rider to put the horse

clearly onto the desired line first before asking for shoulder-in. The horse is then in control before the lateral movement is asked for.

- The rider must be clear in his own mind as to the line he is trying to ride.

AIDS AND EXECUTION

- The aids are as described in the previous exercises.

RELEVANT TEACHING POINTS

- All the teaching points referred to in the last two exercises apply here.
- Encourage the rider to visualise in his mind's eye the line he is going to ride and then set up the shoulder-in along it.
- If necessary the rider may be asked to ride the line in walk or trot so that he is crystal clear about his intention before attempting the shoulder-in.

FAULTS

- The rider may have difficulty maintaining the line from which the shoulder-in is ridden.
- The horse may lose balance, position and confidence through not having the 'support' of the wall.

PART TWO

JUMPING EXERCISES

INTRODUCTION

Training people and horses to jump confidently and competently is as much an art as training the dressage horse and rider. Comparisons can be drawn and common criteria apply. The better the horse is trained on the flat, i.e. basic obedience, suppleness, rhythm, balance, and desire to move forward, the better the horse is likely to perform over fences. The only limitation will then be the horse's mental attitude to wanting to jump fences cleanly.

SETTING UP AND MANAGING THE EXERCISES

The jumping exercises chosen are designed to be managed fairly easily by one instructor working alone. Occasional adjustment of a pole or two for height or the rebuilding of a jump is all that should ever be needed. Major alterations of the fences should not be necessary.

Whilst the building of any grid may take a little time (or less if several pairs of hands can be put to the task), once set up it can be used by others – say, a number of consecutive classes or several groups in one jumping clinic.

Unless otherwise stated, **the distances assume that the exercise is being built in a 20 x 40m school**, on a suitable riding surface. It is important to bear this in mind if an exercise is to be built in a much larger arena or in a field, where longer approaches may render the distances suggested a little short.

UNDERSTANDING DISTANCES

It is important for all instructors to be able to recognise when a distance he has built is not working for one or more horses. Often the instructor blames the distance for being wrong, but it is vital that the instructor is able to decide whether the distance built does not suit a horse because:

(a) the distance really is too long/short for the horse to be able to negotiate it comfortably;

(b) the pace is too idle or too fast for the horse to accommodate the acceptable distance;

(c) the length of the approach (long or short) affects the length of stride at which the horse actually meets the fence;

(d) the going (heavy, slippery, hard) affects the length of stride;

(e) the gradient (uphill or downhill) affects the balance of the horse in the approach to the fence.

It is the instructor's responsibility to learn to use distances in a versatile and efficient way to develop the ability of both horse and rider. Poor use of distances can quickly cause a rider to lose confidence and a horse to become anxious and tense. The quality of the jump will then suffer and the problems become cumulative. If, for instance, shoulder-in or counter canter is badly taught, the horse may become tense or incorrect and the rider may be disillusioned, but rarely will lasting damage be done. Once the rider receives sound help, corrections and improvement will be lasting and effective. But if a rider (and particularly a young impressionable horse) receives poor instruction over fences, damage can be swift and lasting.

Remember: Grid work is beneficial and effective **only** if the instructor on the ground is capable of recognising when distances need adjusting and/or when the rider needs help in how to organise the pace or approach to make the distance appropriate.

EXPECTED ABILITY LEVEL

The following jumping exercises are directed at riders and, to a lesser extent, horses who have established some basic ability over fences. They are not appropriate for novice riders in their early jumping lessons. With the exception perhaps of the first exercise, all the subsequent exercises expect an established jumping position with the balance and control that that should convey.

Novice horses may be worked progressively through these exercises with care, as long as the rider is proficient and experienced in introducing young horses to grid work. Grid work is beneficial and effective **only** if the instructor on the ground is capable of recognising when distances need adjusting, or if the rider needs help in how to organise the pace or approach to make the distance appropriate.

COMPETITIONS

Competitions, particularly affiliated ones (under BE and BSJA rules), lay down distances which are standard for different levels of competitions, with regard to doubles, combinations and related distances. When training an aspiring competition rider, therefore, it is necessary for them to be able to jump these official distances if they are to be safe and successful in competition. However, during training it is vital to develop the confidence and competence of horse and rider through progressive work which correctly builds ability. It may be necessary therefore to reduce competition distances a little when training and also to accommodate those horses and ponies who are never going to have the scope to jump competition distances. Again, the instructor's responsibility is to know when to adapt the distances – when to go shorter and when to go longer.

PREPARATION/WARM-UP

- The riders should work in open order in walk, trot and canter to loosen the horses and prepare them to jump.
- The horse must be well warmed up in walk, trot and canter before starting to jump.
- The type of work that is particularly appropriate to preparing a horse and rider to jump includes: **transitions** both progressive and direct; **turns** and **circles** to supple the horse; **shortening** and **lengthening**, especially in canter, to ensure that the horse is responsive and on the aids.
- The riders should check their girths and make sure their stirrups are comfortable and at a satisfactory jumping length before jumping the first fence.

THE RIDER'S JUMPING POSITION

The rider should have shorter stirrups, with the lower leg secure and under the upper body. The upper body should have a slight inclination forward. The rider's weight should be taken through the thigh and lower leg into the heel. The seat is light, neither fully in the saddle, nor lifted off it. The reins should be shorter, with the hand in a position to allow the horse to stretch his neck in the air over the fence.

IMPORTANT POINTS RELEVANT TO ALL THE JUMPING EXERCISES

- The following exercises can be used for individuals or groups of riders.
- The approach to any fence must be made in open order (in a grid the last rider must have cleared the last element before the next rider starts his approach).
- Use of a grid develops obedience and athleticism in the horse.
- Grid-type exercises help to teach the horse to adjust his stride if differing distances are used, by learning to shorten and lengthen.
- The instructor must always be watching the grid whenever a rider is riding toward it or negotiating it.
- The instructor must encourage his class to take responsibility for their own safety and that of others whilst in a jumping lesson.
- Horses waiting for their turn to jump should be kept quietly moving, if possible.
- In a large group (say, six to eight riders) it is sensible to divide the group into two sections: three or four riders work for a short period, while three or four rest and watch (on the centre line or somewhere else that is safe, e.g. in a corner).

BASIC GRID

Arena
20 x 40m (minimum)

Gaits
approach in trot

Key
njs = non-jumping stride

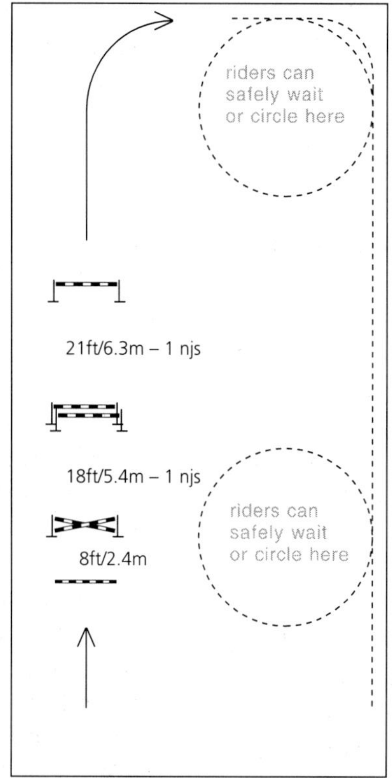

ABOUT THIS EXERCISE

- This exercise should be built up progressively, starting with the placing pole and cross-pole, and adding the subsequent jumps one by one.
- The grid can be built on a threequarter line (inner track) or on the centre line. Note that centre line grids allow approaches from either rein alternately, but that they require much more competence from the rider as the turn demands greater preparation, accuracy and balance from the horse.
- The approach is made in a balanced, rhythmical **trot**.
- The horse makes a trot stride over the placing pole, jumps the cross-pole, takes one non-jumping stride in canter and jumps the second fence.
- After one more non-jumping stride, the horse jumps the last fence and proceeds away from the grid in a straight line in canter.
- Trot can be re-established at any time after the departure from the fence.
- If the corner after the line is taken in canter, balance and rhythm must be maintained before a good downward transition into trot.

AIMS AND BENEFITS

- Approaching fences in trot, especially with a placing pole, helps to ensure that the horse will take off for the first fence in a balanced, controlled way.

- Achieving a balanced, controlled jump into the grid, makes it easier for the horse to progress through the other elements calmly and confidently.
- Jumping from trot generally requires more athleticism than jumping a similar type of fence from canter.
- Grids can help to keep the horse straight in his jumping.
- Grids help to teach the rider to sit still and maintain balance and control.
- Grids help riders to gain confidence in their ability to jump as they do not have to worry about the point of take-off, which will be more assured by the initial placing pole and the subsequent regulated distances.

PREPARATION

- A forward-going, rhythmical trot is essential, but there must be no sense of hurrying the horse.
- A good corner must be ridden so that the horse arrives at the fence straight, going forward and in the middle of the jump, at right angles to it.

AIDS AND EXECUTION

- The rider should approach in a balanced jumping position.
- The trot may be rising or 'sitting', but the latter in a light jumping position.
- The horse is held straight through a co-ordination of the leg and hand aids.
- Depending on the direction of approach, the inside leg and hand will be the right (if on the right rein) the outside hand and leg will be the left.
- The corner is ridden with accuracy and energy to allow the horse to come to the fence straight and balanced.
- The rider maintains contact in the approach, over the fence and on landing, but allows as much stretch through the head and neck over the fence as the horse wishes to take.

RELEVANT TEACHING POINTS

- The group works in open order and comes to the grid in turn.
- Each rider must approach only when the grid is clear, i.e. when no one else is negotiating it.
- There must be room for a fence to be rebuilt if one is knocked down.
- The riders should not be on the long side adjacent to the jump when someone is in the grid.
- Riders should not be in the way of the approach or the departure while someone is trying to approach the grid.
- The instructor must be quick to recognise when the height of the fence or distance(s) need adjusting in the interests of the horse's well being or the rider's confidence.

FAULTS

- The horse may cut the corner in the approach or departure. Check the rider's care and application. A cone can be used to ride around to correct the corner.
- The horse may cut away after the fence and not continue straight. The same correction can apply as for the previous fault.
- The horse may hurry or slow down in the approach.
- The horse may gain too much pace through the grid.
- The horse may drift to the right or left through the grid.

GRID WITH A BOUNCE

Arena
20 x 40m (minimum)

Gaits
approach in trot

Build up the grid progressively

Key
njs = non-jumping stride

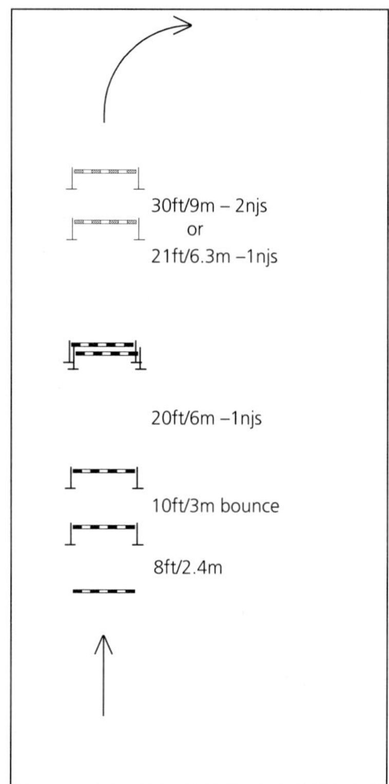

ABOUT THIS EXERCISE

- This exercise should be built up progressively. Start with the placing pole and cross-pole, add a second fence to create a bounce, then bring in the third fence (an oxer), and finally the fourth fence.
- The exercise is best positioned on a threequarter line, although it can be used on the centre line which would enable it to be ridden from an approach on either rein. Note that a centre line approach requires a more competently trained horse and rider.
- The exercise can be set up with either one or two strides between the last element of the grid, depending on space. A two stride element will probably make the approach and departure too short in a 20 x 40 school, whereas two strides can easily be accommodated in 20 x 60m. The diagrams give distances for both one and two strides in the final element.
- The exercise is approached with a placing pole from **trot**.
- The horse takes a trot stride over the placing pole, jumps the first fence and then the second fence without taking a stride between the two obstacles. (This is known as a 'bounce'.)
- The horse then takes one non-jumping stride before jumping the next fence, now from canter. He takes one or two non-jumping strides (depending on the design of the grid) and jumps the final fence.
- The horse makes the departure in canter from

the fence and negotiates the corner in canter before regaining trot in a balanced transition.

AIMS AND BENEFITS

- A bounce requires the horse to be more athletic and supple.
- Prepares horse and rider for the bounce fences so often found on cross-country courses.
- A bounce teaches riders balance and co-ordination – they need to learn to sit and maintain impulsion as there is no non-jumping stride in which to regain lost energy.
- A bounce teaches the horse to be quick and neat, particularly with his front legs.

PREPARATION

- The horse must be going forward with a good rhythm in trot.
- The corner must be ridden with care and accuracy to maintain the quality of the pace.
- The horse must come to the placing pole straight and at right angles to it in the centre.

AIDS AND EXECUTION

- The exercise is ridden in the way described for the previous exercise.
- The horse must be kept straight and active in the trot.

RELEVANT TEACHING POINTS

- If the horse has not negotiated a bounce before it may be wise to build the two elements of the fence as cross-poles, which will keep the horse channelled and central.
- Similarly, for the less experienced rider attempting a bounce for the first time, a cross-pole often appears more inviting.

FAULTS

- All the faults that could occur in the first exercise may be apparent here.
- If the horse is lacking energy in the approach he may stop, feeling he cannot negotiate the bounce.
- In a two-stride final element the horse may make too much or too little ground, in which case the two strides will either ride very short, or 'tight', i.e. not enough room comfortably for two strides – the horse may lose ground and then the strides will ride 'long'. In either case working on the consistency of the canter is the remedy.

DEVELOPING THE BOUNCE GRID

Arena
20 x 40m (minimum)

Gaits
approach in trot

Build up the grid progressively

Key
njs = non-jumping stride

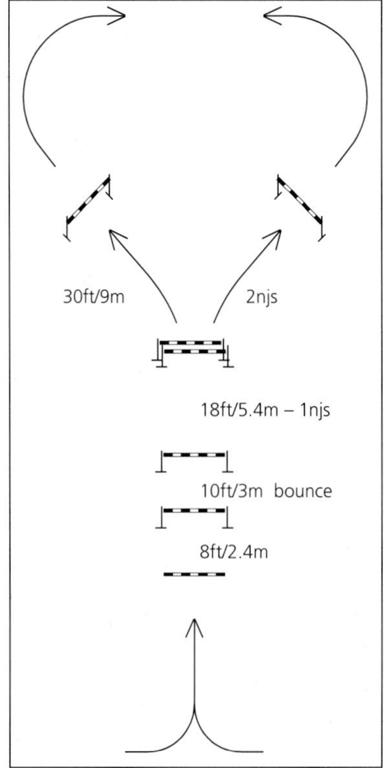

ABOUT THIS EXERCISE

- This exercise should be built up progressively. Start with the placing pole and cross-pole, add a second fence to create a bounce, then bring in the third fence (an oxer), and finally the angled fences.
- The exercise is ridden from **trot**.
- The exercise is positioned on the centre line.
- The approach can be made from either rein.
- The horse approaches straight, in trot; he trots over the placing pole and jumps the first and second element of the grid without taking another stride (a 'bounce').
- One non-jumping stride from canter, still straight, takes the horse to the next fence. On jumping this the horse is smoothly directed left or right and jumps the remaining fence in the direction chosen.
- The distance from the last centre line fence to the angled fence is two non-jumping strides.
- The choice of approach may be from the left and staying to a left-angled fence, in which case the rein is changed in the departure; or the approach may be from the right with a left-handed final fence in which case the exercise finishes again on the right rein. The diagram shows the different options.

AIMS AND BENEFITS

- This exercise requires prior thought from the rider as to the direction he will ask the horse to take from the centre line.

- The exercise requires obedience from the horse to answer the turn from the centre line to the angled fence.
- The exercise requires suppleness and balance to negotiate the last fence after a gentle turn.
- The exercise can develop obedience to both leading legs in canter on the centre line.
- The exercise on page 58 should help prepare the horse for this work.
- The exercise requires a calm, obedient, attentive horse who is responsive to the aids.

PREPARATION

- The horse must be forward going and rhythmical in trot.
- He must maintain balance and impulsion in the turn onto the centre line on both reins.
- He must answer the rider's request to change direction to the final fence with a calm, fluent response.
- The rider must decide in advance which way he will turn from the centre line to the last fence.
- Ideally the turn should be made to left or right alternately, to the leading leg of the canter.
- The rider should dictate the horse's leading leg on the centre line via a very slight positioning of the horse and the application of the correct aids.

AIDS AND EXECUTION

- The balance and positioning of the horse on the centre line and the direction into the turn may dictate which leading leg he takes through the grid.
- The rider can influence the leading leg very carefully through his ability to bend the horse (but keep him straight through his limbs – outside hind tracking outside fore) and the application of the aids for canter (see canter exercises, especially the one on page 58).
- The turn to the final fence must be smooth and in balance so that the horse meets the fence straight and to the centre and is able to make a good effort to jump it.

RELEVANT TEACHING POINTS

- The horse must be making balanced turns onto the centre line without losing the shoulder to the outside before the final element of the grid is added.
- The rider must be encouraged to sit still and in balance and not throw his body weight in the direction he wants the horse to go.
- The turns must come from smoothly applied aids and the horse must be able to respond in harmony.
- Jumping the fence should not be the priority; the manner of getting to the fence is much more important.

FAULTS

- The rider becomes anxious and may find himself in front of the movement, particularly to the last fence.
- The rider may 'pull' the horse around to the last fence rather than riding him with the legs and maintaining his own balance with the horse.
- If the outside shoulder is lost through the turn or on the centre line then the turn to the last fence will be difficult or impossible.
- The horse may be tense and rushed; if so, the turn will reflect this.

CENTRE LINE ZIGZAG

Arena
20 x 40m (minimum)

Gaits
trot, or trot and canter

Build up the grid progressively

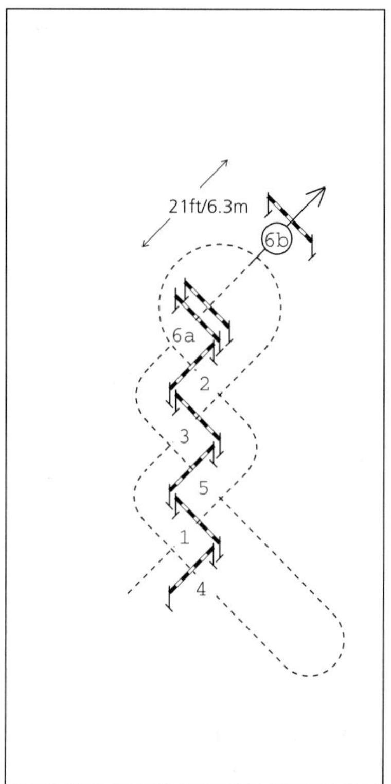

ABOUT THIS EXERCISE

- The zigzag line of fences should be built up progressively in the numerical order shown in the diagram. Note that Fence 6b is an optional double which can be added on to Fence 6 (shown as 6a).
- The fences can be built as small cross-poles, vertical fences or with one or two as spreads, depending on the ability of the group and their horses.
- The exercise can be ridden all from **trot** or a mixture of **trot** and **canter**.
- The rider must be able to negotiate smooth turns from one fence to the next.
- This exercise requires balance and obedience from the horse with supple, fluent turns, and thinking ahead from the rider.

AIMS AND BENEFITS

- The exercise is useful for a group where variation from a grid is required but there is neither time nor space to build a whole course of fences.
- The exercise can remain on the centre line, and if the poles are removed, school movements may be ridden and work continued around the jump wings.
- Despite its complexity, the exercise is easily managed by one instructor with little or no help after the initial construction.

- The exercise develops fluency and suppleness from the horse through making frequent changes of direction from fence to fence.
- To encourage the rider to think ahead, look ahead and ride a good line to each fence.
- The exercise should encourage the horse to maintain rhythm and harmony between fences.
- It is possible to incorporate a double (with one non-jumping stride) after Fence 6 (see Fences 6a and 6b in the diagram).

PREPARATION

- The line of approach to the first fence and each subsequent jump as it is added to the sequence needs to be carefully thought out by the rider, as the lines of approach in this exercise are fairly critical.
- The riders should not (and this applies to any other jumping exercise) follow another rider too closely over a fence in case the fence is knocked down or the first rider has a refusal.
- As the sequence of jumps is built up, the riders should work through the exercise individually. Other riders must not interfere with the one jumping – this may require some riders to stand in the corner from time to time.

AIDS AND EXECUTION

- The emphasis must be on the rider thinking ahead so that the horse is clear about which fence he is approaching.
- The horse must be presented straight to the centre of each fence. An angled approach to any fence will inhibit a straight approach to the next fence.
- The lines of approach and departure to each fence are critical for the successful riding of this exercise.

RELEVANT TEACHING POINTS

- The positioning of the instructor throughout this exercise is important. He must always be able to see the approach and departure of each rider to each fence, but in this exercise he must be sure that he is never in the way of the rider through any of these approaches or departures.
- The fences can be as small or as large as the ability of the horses and riders dictates. If built in a 20 x 60m school the scope for this exercise is much greater.
- Other riders can be kept on the move, certainly in the early build up of the exercise, as long as this is done with judgement and awareness of the one rider who is moving over the fences. As the exercise develops, though, it may be preferable to ask non-jumping riders to stand in a corner and observe until their turn comes.
- If riders are standing still, they should be involved in observing the other riders and learning from them.

FAULTS

- If the lines to each fence are poorly ridden then this will have an accumulative effect on the outcome of the next fence, and so on.
- If the pace deteriorates and the horse rushes, this again will have an effect on the overall exercise.
- The success of this exercise is dependent on all the component parts (each fence built into the whole exercise) being ridden with balance, straightness and control.
- If the horse is considerably stiffer on one side then turns in that direction will be more difficult. Similarly, on the soft side, controlling the outside shoulder to maintain straightness to the fence will be an issue.

Arena
20 x 40m (minimum)

Gaits
trot approach

Build up the grid progressively

Key
njs = non-jumping stride

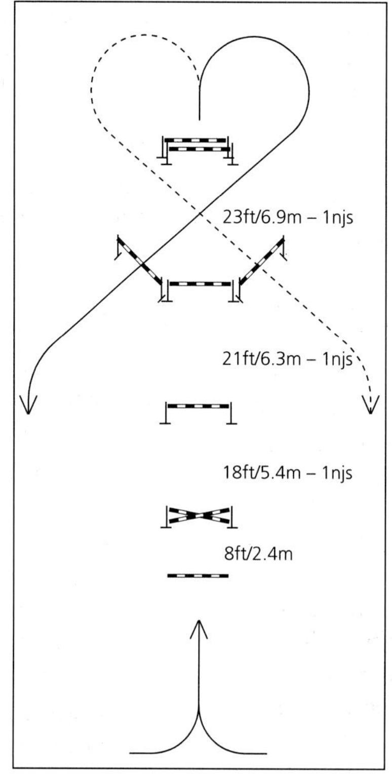

ABOUT THIS EXERCISE

- This exercise should be built up progressively. Start with the placing pole and cross-pole, add the second fence (a vertical), bring in the third fence (another vertical), add on the fourth fence (an oxer) at the end of the line, and finally include the angled fences.
- The exercise makes the same demands on horse and rider as the earlier centre-line grids.
- The initial approach is from **trot**.
- The grid section of the exercise starts and finishes on the centre line and then develops into a test of balance and obedience, requiring suppleness to make a turn either left or right and then jump a fence on the next short diagonal line.
- The exercise can be used easily for groups of riders in a class lesson.

AIMS AND BENEFITS

- The exercise develops suppleness, straightness, obedience and athleticism from the horse.
- The exercise develops confidence, competence, feel and security of position for the rider.

PREPARATION

- The horse must be under control and turn from either rein onto the centre line, while maintaining rhythm and impulsion in the trot.
- The rider must think ahead and ride the turn with energy and awareness.

AIDS AND EXECUTION

- The most important part of riding the grid is to maintain energy through the corner and present the horse straight to the centre of the first placing pole and fence.

RELEVANT TEACHING POINTS

- The instructor must ensure that the riders take full responsibility for staying out of each other's way, particularly allowing room for the person jumping to make a good turn and approach.
- The instructor must always see the approach, jump and departure of every horse at each fence.
- The instructor should avoid giving any verbal assistance (except in an emergency) when the rider is just a few strides away from the fence. At this point, information may be mis-heard, or the instruction is too late for the rider to be able to act on it. Also, attempting to influence the rider too late may have detrimental, rather than beneficial, consequences. It is always better to give advice well before the rider meets a fence.
- The instructor must recognise when the distances between fences are not appropriate and adjust the fences to suit; or, if the distances are acceptable, then teach the rider how to adjust the approach to the fence and the distance between the fences by changing the canter.
- Improving the quality of the jump must be a priority, from an energetic and motivated canter.

FAULTS

- The rider may lose impulsion in the turn onto the centre line or he may lose the horse's shoulder, either through falling in or falling out.
- The horse may, through greenness or lack of confidence, vary his line down the grid by drifting one way or the other.
- Drifting across a fence or wandering off centre in either direction, can make it difficult to maintain the appropriate balance and pace through the grid, and faults are inevitable.
- The distances are not suiting the horse and rider combination.

DOUBLES IN TROT AND CANTER

Arena
20 x 40m or
20 x 60m

Gaits
trot and canter

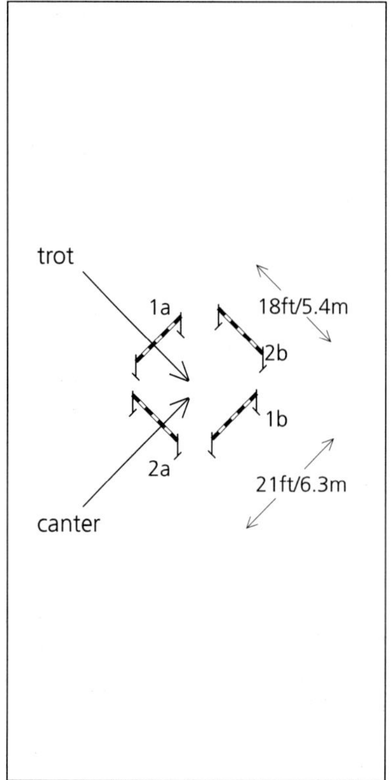

ABOUT THIS EXERCISE

- This exercise, like all the jumping exercises, needs an instructor who is aware of how the distances are working for the horses in the group.
- The exercise can be used in a versatile way if there are varying abilities of horses and riders in the group.
- The floor plan is such that one double is approached from trot and the second double is approached from canter.
- If the group consists of horses and ponies, the ponies could use the 18ft/5.4m distance, approaching in canter, while the horses could approach this in trot.
- Similarly, less competent riders could use the trot distance at a smaller height, while the canter double could be raised for more capable combinations.

AIMS AND BENEFITS

- As described, the exercise can be used for varying of levels of ability and size of equine.
- The distances would be appropriate for school horses working in a quite confined space over relatively small fences (probably up to about 3ft/0.9m).
- For competition training the distances would need to be made slightly greater, although athleticism of the jumping horse is improved by judicial training over short distances.
- Doubles generally improve the suppleness and

co-ordination of both horse and rider.

- Doubles can improve the confidence and jumping ability of horse and rider.

PREPARATION

- The horse and rider should work-in in trot and canter so that they are warmed up and ready to jump.
- The rider needs to maintain a balanced, supple, secure jumping position.
- The rider must be capable of riding straight and in balance to a number of plain fences, preferably both verticals and spreads.
- The combination should make one or two preparatory jumps over a single fence before riding a double.

AIDS AND EXECUTION

- Making the first approach in trot the rider negotiates the trot double with an 18ft/5.4m distance between the two elements. This gives one non-jumping stride.
- The rider concentrates on coming straight to the first element with energy and control, allowing the horse to make the jump in, take one stride and jump out.
- Care must be taken in riding a straight departure.
- The fences may be ridden in open order, provided that the riders maintain awareness of each other and do not approach the double unless the whole combination is clear and not disrupted by a fence being dislodged.
- In riding the canter approach, the rider seeks a balanced, controlled approach, also negotiating the fences with one non-jumping stride.
- The rider needs to develop awareness of the quality of trot or canter which will enable the horse to make a smooth and comfortable jump.
- The rider must pay special attention to the departure from the fence, which must be straight, balanced and in control.

RELEVANT TEACHING POINTS

- The instructor must be in a position to see the jumps at all times, but should not unduly interfere verbally while a rider is making an approach.
- The instructor must be able to offer immediate advice to adjust the pace or the approach to improve the way the horse negotiates the distance.
- The instructor must be able to make immediate adjustment to the distance, if this is necessary, to facilitate the improvement of the horse's way of jumping.
- The instructor must at all times be aware of the confidence and competence of both horse and rider, as this is critical in affecting decisions about altering fence heights or distances.

FAULTS

- The horse may rush as he becomes familiar with the exercise.
- Rushing may be exacerbated by anticipation if following another horse.
- The rider may ride a poor corner or line of approach that could adversely affect the performance over the jump.
- The departure may lack control and balance and this may affect a future approach to another fence.

THE 'COVER-ALL' EXERCISE

Arena
20 x 40m (minimum)

Gaits
trot and canter

Key
njs = non-jumping stride
15ft = 4.5m
18ft = 5.4m
21ft = 6.3m
24ft = 7.2m

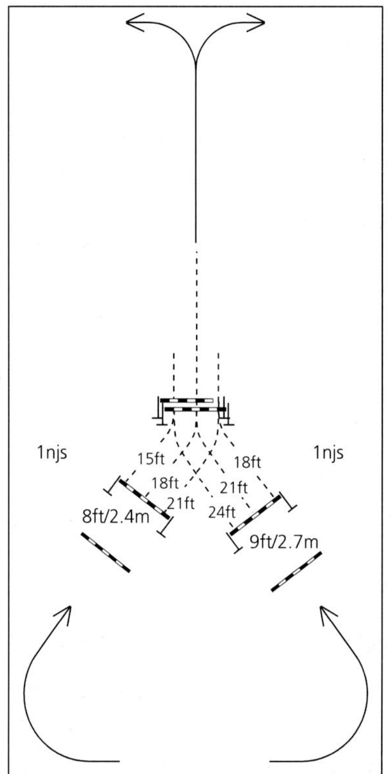

ABOUT THIS EXERCISE

In the author's opinion this is one of the most versatile exercises for a group jumping lesson. I was taught it by Janet Sturrock FBHS, one of the most committed and caring teachers of her time. I have used it more than any other exercise in my lessons with groups of riders.

- The exercise involves one approach from trot and one approach from canter.
- The line through the exercise, either from trot or canter, is then chosen to arrive at the fence on the centre line in an average length of stride, a shorter or longer stride, depending on where the line is ridden, as shown on the diagram.
- The centre fence is jumped and the horse is then ridden straight up the centre line; the left or right rein can be taken depending on the balance of the horse and the direction of the leading leg in the departure.
- This exercise is useful for a group session which includes horses/ponies showing a variety of sizes and lengths of strides.

AIMS AND BENEFITS

- The exercise is very versatile, demanding obedience and suppleness from the horse and thinking ahead and control from the rider.
- The exercise involves making one approach from trot and one from canter, which keeps the horse alert and thinking.

- The exercise taxes the alertness of the rider and also requires him to become quicker in his thinking and in setting up the horse for a tighter corner.
- The exercise has plenty of scope within it to develop shortening and lengthening the stride in trot or canter.
- The line of approach and particularly that up the centre line from the centre fence requires care and accuracy.
- The rider must choose which direction he will turn after the exercise.

PREPARATION

- The riders must be clear about the direction from which they are making the trot approach and which the canter.
- In the canter approach, the transition must be obedient so that the horse is in a balanced gait, thus making the approach easier to ride.

AIDS AND EXECUTION

- The horse must respond to the rider and stay in trot on one rein and then move into canter on command for the second rein.
- The rider should change the rein frequently.

RELEVANT TEACHING POINTS

- The instructor must insist on the exercise being used accurately; it should not deteriorate into a 'free for all', where the regard for the horse and its way of going is of secondary consideration.
- A position closely related to the centre line is preferable to enable the instructor to see all that is happening as it happens.
- Depending on the line ridden, the exercise can teach horse and rider to shorten their canter stride efficiently or conversely to use the range of the canter more effectively and lengthen when desired.

FAULTS

- The rider makes little or no attempt to ride a good line, the fences are then cut across.
- The horse learns the exercise, starts to anticipate and then tends to rush through the fences.

TWO-JUMP CIRCLE

Arena
20 x 40m or
20 x 60m

Gaits
trot and canter

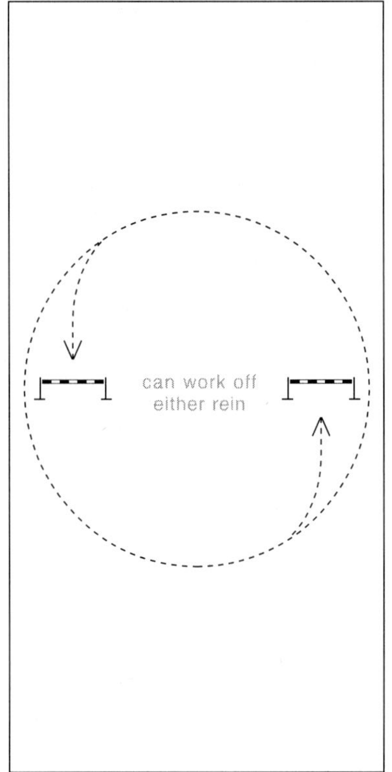

ABOUT THIS EXERCISE

- This exercise involves a 20m circle – it could be larger, if space allows, or smaller, which would make it a more demanding piece of work.
- Two fences are constructed on opposite sides of the circle.
- The fences can be as small or as large as the competence of horse and rider involved dictates.
- The fences can be of any construction but the author would use a straight fence (plain vertical rail) with or without a ground line.
- A plain, straight fence can then be jumped anywhere along its face-line. There is no requirement to be specifically into the centre as, say, a cross-pole would dictate.
- A ground line gives the horse a clearer point of take-off. However, the ground line may be omitted in specific training of the horse, to teach him to improve his judgement and so develop his technique.
- For novices the author would start with a fence of at least 2ft/0.6m – smaller than this and problems can arise because there is not enough height for the horse to actually jump.
- If horse and rider are not capable of jumping at least 2ft/0.6m then the author would not choose this exercise.
- This exercise can usefully be ridden in trot and canter.

AIMS AND BENEFITS

- The object of this exercise is to develop rhythm and feel of balance of pace and stride on a circle in trot and canter.
- The horse should be calm and relaxed in trot and canter on the circle and able to take in the small fences within the rhythm and harmony of his basic gait.
- Horse and rider should be able to develop feel for waiting or moving the stride to each fence to find an optimum take-off point for the jump.
- Due to the continuity of the circle horse and rider should relax into a pattern of repetition, which enables them to develop a balance and harmony to, over and away from a fence.
- The rider can practise a balanced position on a continuous circle.

PREPARATION

- The exercise should be built up progressively, first by riding circles in trot and canter with balance and rhythm.
- When the basic gaits are secure then a fence can be introduced.
- When the circle and one fence can be negotiated harmoniously, then the second fence can be introduced.
- The exercise should be carried out on both reins.

AIDS AND EXECUTION

- Trot and canter on both reins are ridden on a plain circle with no jumps.
- When the first fence is brought in, the rider should be encouraged to maintain a consistent rhythm in trot or canter and to not disturb the stride in the approach to the fence.
- The aim is always to present the horse at the centre of each fence. However, if it is difficult to meet the centre of the fence due to a loss of balance or line, by using straight, plain, vertical fences the jump is still negotiable safely.
- Similarly in the departure (which becomes the approach to the second fence in due course) the rider must aim to re-establish a regular pace, in balance, as soon as possible.
- When the second fence is introduced the same principles apply. The rider aims for rhythm and harmony within the pace, arriving at the fence with energy, balance and straightness so that the horse is in the best possible position to make a good jump.

RELEVANT TEACHING POINTS

- The instructor must decide when to introduce the first and then the second fence, and then if and when the height should be changed.
- Judgement should depend on the fluency of the performance.
- Horse and rider should find a quiet but confident, purposeful harmony to the fences and away.
- The instructor must be quick to recognise a loss of confidence or competence in either horse or rider and act accordingly before damage is done. Always be prepared to adjust a jump to repair lost confidence in horse or rider.

FAULTS

- The horse may quicken to the fence due to its familiarity inducing a casual attitude. The remedy may be to change direction or height of the fence.
- The rider may interfere too much with the pace in the approach.
- The rider may lean inwards or get in front of the horse in his anticipation of the jump.
- Insecurity of the rider's position can cause a loss of balance, particularly in the air (this includes looking down, leaning one shoulder down, swinging the lower leg back or forward, getting in front of the horse or being left behind).
- When linking the two fences together the rider must keep the outside leg in good effect in case the horse tries to fall out on the perimeter of the circle.

SIMPLE RELATED DISTANCES AND 'DOGLEG'

Arena
20 x 40m or
20 x 60m

Gait
canter

Distances = 19 yd/5.7m

Note
The fences can be linked together in the following ways, but they must all be verticals:

1 → 2 or 2 → 1
1 → 4 or 4 → 1
2 → 3 or 3 → 2

Options
Ascending spread fences could be included as long as they are jumped with due regard for the direction of approach

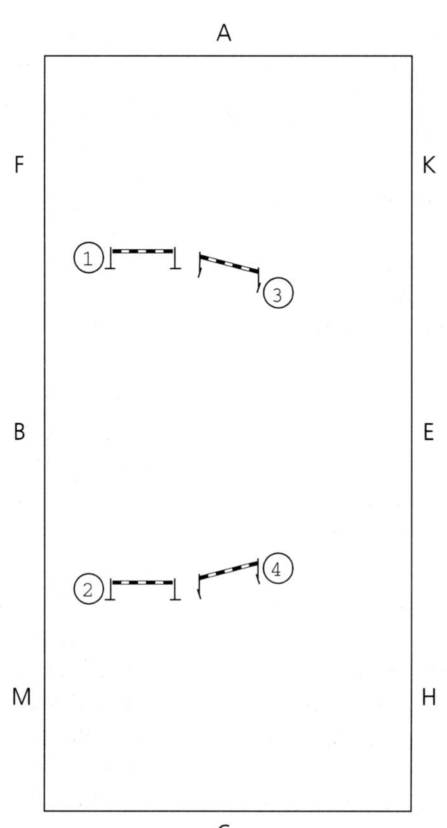

ABOUT THIS EXERCISE

- This exercise should develop the rider's ability to feel the optimum stride of the horse when coming to a fence and therefore the horse's most comfortable point of take-off.
- If using plain vertical fences the jumps can be negotiated in both directions.
- If jumps three and four (see diagram) are to be spread fences these must be jumped in the direction of the ascending oxer face.
- The straight related distance of 19 yards (5.7m) should ride as an easy four strides.
- It should be remembered that these distances are designed for the average school horse working in an indoor school. The instructor must be able to monitor the distances and adjust them if more room is needed for more scopey jumping horses.
- When using the 'dogleg' (from fence 1 to 4, or from fence 3 to 2) the rider must learn to find the line which best suits the horse.
- This exercise can be used for individuals or groups of riders.

AIMS AND BENEFITS

- This exercise teaches both horse and rider to find a good line between two fences.
- Particularly by using the 'dogleg' the rider learns to take a wider or a shorter line to find the optimum point of take-off for the fence.

- On the straight related line, the rider will learn to feel when to 'wait' with the stride and when to 'move' it to enable the horse to maintain a balanced stride or make up a little ground if necessary.
- The use of this exercise helps the rider to feel where the horse naturally loses or gains ground between fences, resulting in an increasing awareness of how to influence the horse to improve its ability to jump, without disrupting balance.

PREPARATION

- The work should start with normal loosening and warming-up procedures prior to any jumping. Additionally it might be helpful to do some shortening and lengthening in canter on one of the long sides of the arena before starting to jump.
- The introductory jump can be over fence 1, first out of trot and then canter. Since this exercise is worked out of canter, the aim is to progress to canter quite swiftly.
- The rider needs to be able to adopt a balanced and secure jumping position.
- The line to each fence must be ridden with care and good preparation.

AIDS AND EXECUTION

- The rider must aim to present the horse at the centre of the fence in the most rhythmical and balanced canter he can muster. Impulsion must be consistent, and the rider must avoid making any last-minute changes that could disturb the take off.
- On the straight-line related distance the rider should be aiming to maintain rhythm and pace on a straight line between the fences.
- Notice should be taken of where the strides vary if the horse does not take four even strides from fence 1 to fence 2.
- When riding the 'dogleg', care must be taken to keep the horse balanced out of the corner in the approach.
- The line of departure from fence to fence (e.g. 1 to 4) must be ridden decisively.

RELEVANT TEACHING POINTS

- The instructor must always be alert and watching whenever a rider is negotiating a fence.
- The instructor must take responsibility for adjusting any distance immediately it becomes obvious that it is not suiting a horse.
- The instructor should be in a safe position that enables him to see the whole performance, not in the way of the horse and rider.
- It is advisable to keep instructions to the rider to a minimum, especially when the rider is negotiating the fences. Comments should be made after the performance, as it will then be easier for the rider to assimilate them and act on them in future work.
- The instructor must decide when to raise the fences in order to develop the work appropriately.

FAULTS

- The horse may make too much ground through the related strides.
- Conversely, he may not make enough ground to take the required number of regular strides.
- In each case the instructor must be able to advise the rider on how to deal with the problem to improve it, or decide that the fences must be changed.
- The rider may ride a poor line that adversely affects the related distance.

ALSO AVAILABLE

Learning to ride should be fun, progressive and constructive, but all too often children can be frightened or put off. Teaching them is not easy.

For everyone teaching 4–12-year-olds at riding schools, clubs or at home, **Teaching Children to Ride** offers advice, exercises, lesson plans, games and teaching tips designed to provide variety and sound instruction, plus a fund of innovative ideas for making learning to ride an enjoyable, worthwhile and satisfying experience, even for the very young.

It includes advice on – planning a lesson • teaching the basics • starting and finishing lessons • mid-lesson breaks • fun exercises for early lessons • trotting • using poles • cantering • introducing jumping • advanced work for older children • riding out • mounted games.

Jane Wallace, a former international three-day event rider, is a well known author, respected trainer and mother of two pony-mad sons.